PETERSON'S

SAT*

WORD FLASH

The Quick Way to Build Verbal Power for the New SAT—and Beyond

Joan Carris

*SAT IS A REGISTERED TRADEMARK OF THE COLLEGE ENTRANCE EXAMINATION BOARD, WHICH WAS NOT INVOLVED IN THE PRODUCTION OF, AND DOES NOT ENDORSE, THIS PRODUCT.

Visit Peterson's Education Center on the Internet (World Wide Web) at
www.petersons.com

Library of Congress Cataloging-in-Publication Data

Carris, Joan.
  SAT word flash : the quick way to build verbal power for the SAT—and beyond / Joan Carris.—2nd ed.
    p.   cm.
  Includes index.
  ISBN 0-7689-0505-2
  1. Scholastic Aptitude Test—Study guides.   2. English language—Examinations—Study guides.   3. Vocabulary tests—Study guides.   I. Title.
LB2352.57.C367   1997
378.1′662—dc21   97-8917
                                                                      CIP

Printed in Canada

10 9 8 7 6 5 4 3 2 1

CONTENTS

VITAL INFORMATION

This is not another boring introduction. The next few pages really DO contain vital information, just as the heading says.

Do You Need to Pump Up Your Vocabulary?

Most people would like a big, strong vocabulary for about a zillion reasons, only one of which is needing an impressive SAT or PSAT score. And don't let anyone kid you—the verbal sections on SATs and PSATs are *vocabulary tests*. (So are most IQ tests.)

Remember that your language doesn't just say who you are, it *trumpets* who you are. Either you sound bright and well educated or you don't. You can't fool people—not for long anyway. There is no substitute for an educated vocabulary. Your language will shape your life; I absolutely guarantee it.

Honest Talk About Learning

When you're very young, learning happens all the time, and you don't even have to think about it. One day you're popping those little bits of cereal into your mouth, and the next day your saying "Cheerio, Cheerio!" and a proud parent is grinning from ear to ear. Nothing to it.

Well, you're older now, and the truth is that most learning involves work. The more complex the subject, the more work it's apt to take. **But vocabulary is one of the EASIER things to learn if you go about it the right way.** Isn't that a relief? Also, people remember what they enjoy studying. We tried to build a great deal of FUN into this book.

Analyze Yourself. How Do You Learn?

Ask yourself these few questions. Then you can use the answers to make learning the words in this book easier.

- *Do you learn best in the early morning?* What an awful thought. Still, half the world is like this.
- *Do you learn better in the late afternoon?* In the evening? When are you too sleepy to work well?
- *Do you learn best with music on or off?* Be careful here. Most of us learn well only when it's quiet.
- *Do you need to write something down to learn it?* I would have flunked history if I hadn't highlighted lines in the textbook and written a full outline of all we studied.
- *Do you need to hear something to remember it?* Over one third of us learn best through our ears.
- *Do you feel better about studying if you have iced tea or Coke*, etc., to keep you company?

1

- *Is learning more apt to happen if you work with a friend* or study group, or do you work best alone?
- *Do you learn more efficiently if you say* "I'm going to do this assignment in 30 minutes, no matter what"?

Think about all these topics. Where and when and how do you do your very best learning? You need to know.

Why Learn the Words in This Book?

The words in this book are the *must know* words for SATs. As an SAT/PSAT coach, I've been keeping records for fifteen years of the words that stump kids over and over again. Those words are all here. On the SATs published since 1980, certain words occur regularly. THOSE WORDS are here, too.

Why do the same words appear again and again in most SAT prep books and on tests similar to SATs? Because these particular words really do the job. They are some of our most descriptive, specific adjectives—our most precise, active verbs—our information-packed nouns—yet none is overused or trite.

Words used all the time lose their punch. Let's take *sad*. Sara is sad about losing her boyfriend. Does that give you a vivid picture of Sara? No, and that's why we need *downcast, gloomy, sorrowful, disheartened, morose, anguished, wretched,* and all the others, each with its separate shades of meaning, so that we know EXACTLY how Sara feels.

Who Needs This Many Words?

You do, if you want to go to college or if you want to be thought of as an intelligent person. Remember that you must have a respectable vocabulary to be a good reader, and about 90 percent of college work depends on reading comprehension. Also, competence in writing is required in college and on the job, and *only* good readers are good writers. Since you need to be a good reader AND writer (let's add good speaker too), a bigger vocabulary is obviously the first requirement.

Remember, too, that your aim in talking and writing is to communicate, not in a general way but very specifically. Accurate communication requires a large supply of words. If your boss asks you to analyze progress on a project, he won't appreciate "It's going, like, kinda okay, you know?"

Even if you're a math major or a computer techie, you'll need to communicate your knowledge effectively and persuasively to other people. Einstein had to explain to others the significance of $E = mc^2$.

Enough! you're hollering. Okay, because even if I gave you a hundred reasons for learning these words, it would still boil down to the real reason: *lifestyle choice.* Strong language skills will get you the job, and therefore the lifestyle that you want. Lousy language skills will limit your choices alarmingly.

So, think . . . Where do you want to go in life and how will you get there? We're agreed that an educated vocabulary is the first step. Now, how can you get one with a minimum of agony?

How to Learn Every Word in This Book

First, fire up your determination. People who make things happen are determined people. Just wishing is never enough. If it were, you'd have a Porsche in your driveway.

Next, *try what I'm suggesting here.* Then, if it doesn't work, make your own plan for mastering these lists. We're only talking about 400 to 500 words, depending on how many synonyms you learn along the way.

1. **Flip through the book to get a feel for each lesson.** There are thirty lists of words, only twelve words each, plus two roots and their necessary words, for a total of sixteen words in each lesson. You'll know at least a couple on each list, so you'll actually be learning fourteen words at most. Every five lists, there's a review lesson to make sure you still know the words.

2. **Try this Three-Day Miracle Plan for each lesson:**

   Day 1—Read each word, its definition, and the example sentences. Read all the way through, because often a story will lead you from one word to the next. Concentrate on any word that seems hard to remember. After studying the roots and their example words, do Memory Fix, the first practice with words in each lesson.

   Day 2—Do the rest of the exercises. Write in this book. Highlight. Underline. Check any questions about pronunciation in a collegiate dictionary like *Webster's* or *Random House.*

   Day 3—Self-quiz. Write the new words on a separate piece of paper with a definition or synonyms for each. If you know them all, rent a movie with friends to celebrate. Tomorrow you can begin a new list.

3. **You'll need just a few minutes a day** for three months to learn every word in this book on our Three-Day Miracle Plan. That's just one summer—or late summer and early fall. If you can work faster, do it. If you're a slow worker, it would be smarter to learn fewer words thoroughly, so that you have them for life, rather than trying to cram in all the words, retaining hardly any.

4. **If you learn best in a group, form an SAT study group** with regular meeting times and assignments. Medical students do this to learn their most difficult subjects, and you can, too. Group learning is usually fun.

5. **Read . . . and read some more.** Nothing helps people to learn words like seeing them in context over and over again. (People who love to read always think SAT verbal sections are easy.) If you come across a word you don't know, ask someone who does, then *write the word and its definition in this book.* Or look up the unknown word in a dictionary.

   Read magazines or newspapers that are well written, such as *Sports Illustrated, The New York Times,* the *Christian Science Monitor*, the *Boston Globe*, the *Washington Post*, etc.

Read books on topics you enjoy. If it isn't pleasurable, you won't do it. Reading is supposed to be fun.

6. **Yes, use the dictionary.** It's your friend, and you need to have a solid relationship. Get a pocket dictionary to carry with you. All bright people act this way.

7. **Limit your TV time.** Unless you're trying to beef up your total of 18,000+ murders seen by graduation (the average for all high schoolers), punch the little OFF button and let the boob tube rest. Its vocabulary *stops* at the sixth-grade level, remember?

8. **Think about opposites.** Antonyms are useful memory tools. *Night* has much more meaning when contrasted with *day*. If you know that *joyful* is the opposite of *morose*, you'll remember what *morose* means even though you use it less often.

9. **Think about roots.** The etymology (word history + root) of a word is a vital clue to its meaning. You know that a *hydr*ant dispenses *water.* So if you *hydr*ate a substance, you're adding water. An an*hydr*ous compound has no water . . . and so on. Knowing roots is the key to the meaning of 60 to 70 percent of English words.

   Every root you learn is a kind of verbal gold. A root like *duc/duct* (lead, guide) is the basis for over 2,000 English words. *Gen* in *gen*tleman, *gen*esis, and in*gen*uous has spawned over 50 words, all of them favorites with SAT question-makers. *The roots you absolutely must know are in this book, two solid-gold roots per lesson.*

10. **How can you remember all the words?** Make flashcards. If law and medical students do it, then we should pay attention. Smart people do what works. Ask parents and friends to quiz you with the flashcards. Carry them with you in your pocket or purse. You'll be astounded at what you can learn in a few odd minutes here or there.

Use memory aids to fix words in your mind. These are called *mnemonic devices.* Mne = *memory* as in *a*mnesia, *a*mnesty, and *mne*monics. (See what I mean about roots?) Draw a picture on your flashcards if it helps. Connect a person to a word. Make a silly sentence using the word you need to memorize. *Brusque Bob Baker barks at me.* Mnemonics work best when they're personal.

Another great memory aid is writing. The old schoolmarm trick of "Write it ten times" was a trick that worked. It still does.

Try all this, okay? If you're not learning words like crazy after a few weeks, devise methods that you like better. In other words, move through this book at your own pace, in your own way. You're acquiring an educated vocabulary to use the rest of your life. And while you're learning the new words, *use them!* That's the only way to keep them forever.

WHAT YOU ALREADY KNOW— A QUICK REVIEW

Promise. This *will* be quick because you already know these critical bits of vocabulary. Just whip through this review, and you'll feel much happier about your vocabulary. These are terribly helpful clues to thousands of English words that you need, and you *really do know them*. They've just been hanging around in the back of your mind, waiting for you to call on them.

The two lessons here will take only 30 minutes each—probably the best hour you'll spend all week. *You're going to be amazed* at what you already know that will boost your score on any test involving words.

Lesson A

How do smart people learn? They write information down, read what they've written, and say it out loud. They may repeat these three steps a few times, fixing the material in mind, and then they'll have it forever. So, get smart! Write these roots down, learn their definitions and those of the sample words, and you'll be taking a large step toward a bigger vocabulary.

AQUA and HYDR = water and MAR = sea, ocean

aquarium	hydrant	marine
aqualung	hydraulic	aquamarine
aquamarine	dehydrate	mariner
aqueduct	hydrolysis	maritime
	hydrogen	submarine

So *aquamarine* (a pale turquoise-colored stone) really means "water of the sea," a perfect description.

EGO and AUTO = I, self

ego	autocrat
egotist	autograph
superego	automobile
egocentric	autobiography
alter ego	autonomous
	autodidactic

BIO = life

biology biopsy biography

autobiography symbiosis

MATER = mother and **PATER = father**

matron	paternal
maternal	patriot
matrimony	paternity
matriarchal	patriarchal
maternity	patrimony

A *patriot*, therefore, is loyal to his *father*land.

AUD/AUDIT = hear

audition audible auditorium

inaudible audience audit

SCRIB/SCRIPT and **GRAPH/GRAM = to write**

scribe	graphic
scribble	telegraph
inscribe	biography
describe	photography
prescribe	telegram
proscribe	mammogram
inscription	cardiogram
description	

My *auto-bio-graphy*, the story of my life, is literally "writing my life." Three roots in one word.

GE/GEO = earth and **AGR = field, soil**

geology	agriculture
geophysics	agronomy
geometry	agrarian
apogee	agrochemical

SCI and COGN/COGNI/GNO(S) = to know

science	cognizant
omniscient	cognate
prescient	incognito
conscious	recognize
	prognosis
	agnostic

Prescient . . . a tough word, right? Not anymore. The prefix *pre* meaning "before" and the root *sci* give you the meaning. *Prescient* means "knowing ahead of time, able to foretell."

VID/VIS = to see

video	evident
provide	vision
revise	advise
improvise	

CHRON and TEMPOR = time

chronology	tempo
synchronize	temporize
chronometer	temporary
anachronism	contemporary
	extemporaneous

SENS/SENT = to feel

sensible	resent
dissent	consent
sensual	presentiment

A *presentiment* is "a foreboding," a "feeling before" something happens that you know what's about to happen. Another gift from the world of roots!

CIV = citizen

civic	civil
civilian	civilization
civility	

FALL/FALS = to deceive, be not truthful

fallacy	fallacious
infallible	false
falsify	falsehood

Words from this root are *always* on SATs and PSATs!

CYCL = circle

cycle	recycle
cyclical	tricycle
bicycle	Cyclops

NEG = to deny, not

negative	renege
renegade	abnegation

And remember these incredibly useful prefixes? Read each one aloud slowly as a memory refresher.

A/AN = not, without

anomaly	atrophy
amoral	agnostic
atheist	anonymous
amorphous	atypical

AB/ABS = from, away

absent	abhor
abstain	abrupt
abbreviate	abrasive
abdicate	abnormal

(You knew you wanted to stay *away* from someone who was acting *ab*normal, right?)

AC/AD/AF, etc. = to, toward, against

adhere	aggregate
addict	apportion
aspect	attend

ANTE/ANTI = before, previous

anteroom	anticipate	antedate
antecedent	antebellum	anterior

ANTI = against, opposing

antisocial   antithesis   antidote
antiseptic   antipathy   antibiotic

BENE = good, well

benefit   beneficial
beneficent   benefactor
benediction   benevolent

CIRCU = around

circuit   circuitous
circumspect   circumnavigate
circumvent   circumference

CO/COL/COM, etc. = with, together

collateral   cooperate   concede
coerce   collaborate   compassion
correlate   concur

CONTRA/COUNTER = against, opposing

contradict   counteract   countereffective
contraband   contrary

DI/DIA = across, apart, through, between

dilate   diaphragm
diameter   diaphanous
dialogue   dialectic

DIS/DI/DIFF = away, apart, negative

disparate   difference
diffuse   dissuade
disseminate   disperse

EN/EM = in, among, within

enliven   empathy   enhance
embarrass   embed   enforce

MEMORY CHECK

To fix these important prefixes in your memory, fill in the missing info in this chart.

Prefix	Meaning	Examples
A/An		atheist, anomaly, atypical
	from, away	
DIS/DI/DIFF		
	before, previous	anteroom, anticipate
BENE		
	around	
		diameter, dialogue, dilate
ANTI		
	against, opposing	
CO/COL/COM		cooperate, concede, concur

Lesson B

. . . because you can never know too many prefixes!

EPI = outside, over, outer

epilogue   epidermis   epitaph
epiphany   epicenter

EX/EXTRA/EXTER/EXTRO = out, outside, beyond

expel   extrovert   external
extol   extraordinary

HETERO = other

heterodox   heterogeneous   heterosexual

HOMO = same

homogeneous   homophone   homosexual
homonym

IN/IL/IM/IR = in, within or not, opposing

internal   imply   indecent
intrinsic   imprint   inefficient
influx   irradiate   illegal
irreverent

INTER = among, between

interact   intervene   interdict   intersect

INTRA/INTRO = inwardly, within

intramural   intravenous   introduce   introvert

A wee cheer here for roots and prefixes. One who turns (*vert*) himself *out* for others (an outgoing personality) is an *extro*vert; the *intro*vert is turned *in*ward (may be an *intro*spective type), a less open individual by far.

MACRO/MAG/MEGA/MAX = big, long

macrocosm   macroeconomics
magnitude   magnanimous
maximum   megalomaniac

MAL = bad, badly

malady	malicious	malign
malevolent	maleficent	malinger
dismal	malaise	

META/MET = change of, over, beyond

metaphor	metabolism
metaphysics	metamorphism
metastasize	

MEMORY CHECK 1

Try your hand at completing the following sentences.

1. The elephant wears his *epi*dermis on the _____.

2. A *hetero*geneous group is _____.

3. A naked ghost would be both _____decent *and* _____sub-stantial, right?

4. Playing it to the *max* means _____.

5. We know *Male*ficent means trouble in "Sleeping Beauty" because she has such a _____ name.

6. Our favorite *meta*morphic critter is the butterfly, who _____ his form (*morph*) into one that can fly.

MICRO = small

microbe   microscope   microphone   microcosm

OMNI and PAN = all, entire

omnivorous	panorama
omnipresent	panacea
omniscient	pandemic
	pandemonium
	pantheon

ORTH = straight, right

orthodox   orthodontist   orthopedic   orthotics

PAR/PARA = beside, next to

paradox	paragon
parenthesis	paraphrase
paradigm	parasite

PER = through, throughout or completely, wrongly

persecute	permeate
perjury	permit
perturb	persiflage

PERI = around, near

perimeter   periscope   peripatetic   periphery

POST = after, following

postpone   posthumous   postmortem   posterior

PRE = before

predict	prefix
preordained	preliminary
pregnant	precipitate
precocious	predilection

PRO = for, forward, before, forth, favoring

progress	promote
progenitor	prognosis
provision	promise

RE/RETRO = back, again

recoil	retreat
retain	retroactive
retrospect	recur
refer	rehearse
reiterate	remember

MEMORY CHECK 2

As before, fill in the missing boxes in the chart.

Prefix	Meaning	Examples
	small	microbe, microphone, microcosm
PRE		predict, prefix, preliminary
	straight, right	
PER		permeate, permit
	around, near	periscope, perimeter, periphery
PRO		
	after, following	
		recoil, retreat, retroactive
OMNI, PAN		

SE = apart, away from

seclude	segregate
secede	sequester
seduce	separate

SUB/SUC/SUF/SUG/SUM/SUP/SUS = under, below

subzero	submarine
succeed	suffuse
suggest	summon
suppose	suspend

SUPER/SUR = over, above, extra

superstar	superimpose
survey	surpass
superficial	surmount

SYL/SYM/SYN/SYS = together

syllable	symmetry
symphony	synergy
synopsis	synthesis
system	systolic

TELE = from afar

telegram   telephone   telephoto   telescope   telemetry

TRA/TRANS = across, beyond

traverse	travesty
trajectory	transport
transgress	transform

UN and IN = not, opposing

unwary	unequal
unmitigated	unsuspecting
indistinct	inequitable

WITH = against

withhold   withstand   withdraw

MEMORY CHECK 3

Time to put your knowledge of these prefixes to the test. Fill in the blanks in the following sentences.

1. If you *se*clude a criminal in order to *se*gregate him from society, you have _____ him from normal life.

2. A *tele*phone brings you voices from _____.

3. That long, cigar-shaped ship that stays "under the sea" for months at a time is rightly called a _____.

4. A _____ store will provide _____ savings that will _____pass your wildest dreams. These stores truly are *over* and *above* all others, offering many *extras*.

5. The purpose of _____chronizing our watches is so that we will be _____ in time (*chron*).

Answers for this chapter begin on page 196.

A LAUDABLE LIST OF VERBS

acquiesce • chastise • augment • condone • amass • disseminate • coalesce • concur • digress • laud • disperse • efface

ACQUIESCE v. *to give in and agree peaceably; to assent, comply* n. acquiescence
When Dad set 1 a.m. as our curfew, my sister Amy and I *acquiesced* because we knew he meant business. For me, it's easier to *acquiesce* than to argue forever, which I hate.

CHASTISE v. *to scold severly or punish; castigate, censure*
Every day we *chastise* Dude, my insanely brave, five-pound Yorkshire terrier. But Meatloaf, Amy's sixteen-pound cat, has almost never been *chastised*, probably because she's too smart to get caught.

AUGMENT v. *to increase; to make something greater or bigger*
Dad said, "Ted, I'll *augment* your allowance for your senior year, in return for more help at home." That could mean major labor, but I have to *augment* my savings before college.

CONDONE v. *to overlook or pardon an offense; to excuse*
For too long, our family has *condoned* Dude's mad-dog tendencies. We keep making excuses for him, unlike my high school principal, who rarely *condones* misbehavior.

AMASS v. *to accumulate, collect; to gather, come together*
I don't need to *amass* a huge fortune, but a bit of extra money would be nice—for camping gear, of course. Whenever ours is *amassed* in one place, I see how much we need.

DISSEMINATE v. *to disperse or spread everywhere (knowledge or ideas) as if sowing seeds*
Our school paper, *The Central Times*, tries to *disseminate* the information all students need. As editor, I hope the paper also *disseminates* the spirit of Central High.

17

CUR/CURR/COURS = to run, course

cursory—*sketchy, not thorough; hasty or superficial*
a *cursory* glance
a regrettably *cursory* reading

precursor—*a forerunner that hints at the future; harbinger*
the first robin, a welcome *precursor* of spring

Also: **cursive, excursion, current, curriculum, discourse, incur, cursor, occur, concur, discursive**

COALESCE v. *to mix or come together from separate elements*
Thoughts about my last editorial finally *coalesced* into one good idea. Amy couldn't believe I was actually writing about her play cast, a group of radically different kids that I saw *coalescing* into a supportive stage family.

CONCUR v. *to agree, assent; to approve; to coincide*
After much discussion, our family *concurred* on a camping site for next summer. Luckily, Dad's vacation time is *concurrent* with the best time to visit the park we selected.

DIGRESS v. *to wander off course in speaking or writing*
I often *digress* into related topics as I get into a speech. I think these *digressions* are humorous, but my teacher has started saying, "Ted, if you keep *digressing*, I'll mark you down. You must stay on target."

MISS/MIT = to send

emit—*to voice; to give off, as fumes or anger*
emitted a low groan
emit foul fumes
emission standards

mission—*a definite job or task; the mission establishment itself (usually religious)*
needing a clear *mission*
the old adobe Jesuit *mission*

Also: **omit, omission, commit, commission, permit, permission, transmit, transmission, missive, missile**

LAUD v. *to praise, commend, acclaim, extol*
We rarely say, "You are to be *lauded* for that achievement" anymore, favoring the word praised or commended instead. But I often hear "What a *laudable* accomplishment."

DISPERSE v. *to spread all over; to disseminate;* also, *to fan out or scatter in a random way*
With promotion of school events as one goal, we *disperse* copies of *The Central Times* to each class. Most kids came to the recent basketball tournament and *dispersed* like so many bats afterward, flitting home to study for exams.

EFFACE v. *to erase or obliterate; to wear away (as by time)*
I'm counting on time to *efface* the memories of when I've made a total idiot of myself, just as weather has gradually *effaced* the harsh or exaggerated features of nature.

List of Abbreviations

Take a minute to familiarize yourself with the following abbreviations, which are used in the vocabulary lessons.

n.	noun	**s.**	singular	**L.**	Latin
v.	verb	**pl.**	plural	**Fr.**	French
adj.	adjective	**usu.**	usually	**Sp.**	Spanish
adv.	adverb	**lit.**	literally	**Gr.**	Greek
				Ger.	Germanic

MEMORY FIX

To learn these new words, write each one on a sheet of paper. Also write a synonym or definition for each and say the words aloud as you work.

FILL IN THE BLANKS

From the words in this chapter, select the one that best completes the meaning and logic of each phrase below. Note which tense or form of the word is required for sense.

1. wouldn't _____ unless I could yield with a clear conscience

2. can't possibly _____ that rude behavior

3. harsh weather that _____ the writing on the tomb

4. formal enough to say _____ instead of scold

5. an opinion that fortunately _____ with mine

6. "all glory, _____, and honor" goes the hymn

7. to _____ as much as possible, the goal of Scrooge McDuck

8. eager to _____ the number of qualified students

9. careful to focus on the problem and not _____

10. a thorough reading, please, not a _____ one

11. a rambling, _____ talk that put everyone to sleep

12. where the two paths _____ into one wider path

13. hope to _____ the news to as many as possible

14. quit milling around and _____ peaceably now

15. _____ a low cry of astonishment before falling silent

ANALOGIES

Circle the one word pair in each list below that expresses the same relationship as the pair in capital letters.

1. CHASTISE : MISBEHAVIOR
    (A) start : argument
    (B) castigate : students
    (C) laud : success
    (D) represent : hope
    (E) remunerate : reward

2. FOOTPRINTS : EFFACE
    (A) scars : hide
    (B) gulley : widen
    (C) target : omit
    (D) memorial : dedicate
    (E) record : obliterate

3. **ACQUIESCE : YIELDING**
   - (A) comply : hesitating
   - (B) disperse : scattering
   - (C) concur : running
   - (D) emit : smelling
   - (E) commit : halting

4. **PATH : STRAY**
   - (A) lecture : digress
   - (B) book : review
   - (C) illness : recur
   - (D) duties : remiss
   - (E) elements : coalesce

5. **PARDON : OFFENSE**
   - (A) amass : wealth
   - (B) punish : wrongdoing
   - (C) condone : error
   - (D) censure : actions
   - (E) disseminate : cheer

MATCHING

Circle the two words or phrases that best explain the meaning of each of the words in bold type.

1. **acquiesce**
   - (A) dispute
   - (B) assent
   - (C) drench
   - (D) yield

2. **emit**
   - (A) utter
   - (B) voice
   - (C) take in
   - (D) abhor

3. **castigate**
   - (A) scorn
   - (B) chastise
   - (C) scold
   - (D) tie up

4. **precursor**
   - (A) forerunner
   - (B) patron
   - (C) arbiter
   - (D) harbinger

5. **amass**
   - (A) ritual
   - (B) accumulate
   - (C) gather
   - (D) Southern for "disaster"

6. **augment**
   - (A) enlarge
   - (B) add to
   - (C) alter
   - (D) price

7. **disperse**
   - (A) avoid
   - (B) strew around
   - (C) arrange
   - (D) disseminate

8. **coalesce**
   - (A) join
   - (B) roil around
   - (C) come together
   - (D) disturb

9. **efface**
   (A) embarrass
   (B) wear away
   (C) erase
   (D) expose

10. **cursory**
    (A) sketchy
    (B) cautious
    (C) ignorant
    (D) hasty

Answers for this chapter begin on page 197.

DOWN WITH BOMBAST!

---

banal • terse • raconteur • euphemism • succinct•
hackneyed • bombast • articulate • laconic •
hyperbole • lampoon • platitude

BANAL adj. *commonplace and stale, not fresh; trite, insipid*
n. **banality**
Banal, overused phrases and words are so numerous that it's hard to avoid them. Those of us who work on the *Times* cut these *banalities* from every article, including our own, because *banal* means boring, every time.

TERSE adj. *stripped of all but the essentials; concise or succinct, sometimes to the point of rudeness*
When you need encouragement, a *terse* response is disappointing. For instance, that small, *terse* "B" on my history paper seemed like a stingy answer to my weeks of research.

RACONTEUR n. *gifted talker or storyteller*
My English lit class read *The Importance of Being Earnest* by Oscar Wilde, a talented playwright, poet, and *raconteur* who, because he was so amusing, was an extremely popular guest. Wilde died in poverty in Paris; when a friend offered him champagne on his deathbed, Wilde remarked, "I am dying beyond my means."

EUPHEMISM n. *the use of a "nice" word or phrase instead of an offensive or terrible honest one; the word or phrase so used*
My last editorial was on the *euphemism* "ethnic cleansing," a phrase used to disguise the murders in Bosnia-Herzegovina and Rwanda. I enjoy some common *euphemisms*, such as "precocious" (spoiled brat) or "made redundant" ("fired" in Britain), but using a *euphemism* to cloak genocide is revolting.

VOC/VOK = to call

vociferous—*loudly, persistently vocal; clamorous*
the *vociferous* wail of a hungry baby
a *vociferous* message

equivocal—*open to two interpretations, evasive, unclear*
a puzzling, *equivocal* answer
an *equivocal*, uneasy reply

Also: **provoke, provocative, vocal, equivocate, evoke, evocative, invoke, invocation, revoke**

SUCCINCT adj. *brief, to the point; concise, pithy, terse*
Some critics favor the taut, *succinct* writing style of Hemingway or Cather. I enjoy a more colloquial style, like Mark Twain's in *Huckleberry Finn*. For the school paper, of course, we demand *succinct*, pithy articles.

HACKNEYED adj. *banal, overused, commonplace, trite*
The *hackney* was a breed of horse used to pull the old public coaches in England. From their regular, boring routine came the words *hackneyed* and *hack*.

BOMBAST n. *high-flown, pompous, "windbag" language*
The windy, *bombastic* mayor of our town likes to give speeches. Whenever he comes to school, this Bard of *Bombast* yaks away, one empty paragraph after another.

LOC/LOQU/LOG/OLOGY = speech, study, word, talk

eloquent—*extremely expressive (a gesture or words)*
a moving, *eloquent* speech
the *eloquent* bowing of his head

loquacious—*extremely talkative; gabby, garrulous*
a *loquacious* parrot
the *loquaciousness* born of loneliness

Also: **elocution, soliloquy, colloquial, prologue, epilogue, tautology** *(redundancy)*, **eulogy, psychology, biology**

ARTICULATE v. *to speak in a clear, effective way* adj. *clear and effective in manner;* also, *jointed or marked off (as "the beetle's* articulated *segments")*
Amy practices a lot, trying to *articulate* her lines perfectly. I admit that she's a really *articulate* performer, but life with an actress is hard to take.

LACONIC adj. *using as few words as possible; concise*
The old Greek Spartans from the area Laconia were big-deed-doers, not talkers, and came to be known as *laconic* folk. The most *laconic* communication I've heard was between Victor Hugo, author of *Les Miserables*, and his publisher. After the book came out, Hugo wrote: ? His publisher replied: !

HYPERBOLE n. *wild exaggeration, often on purpose for effect*
Reading Twain is fun, partly because he uses *hyperbole* so well. So does the cast on *Saturday Night Live*. The crazy exaggeration of *hyperbole* is probably as much fun for the actors as it is for their audience.

LAMPOON n. *verbal ridicule of a person; personal satire* v. *to ridicule*
The cast of *Saturday Night Live* loves to *lampoon* political figures, especially the president. They let their *lampooning* go as far as TV standards will allow.

PLATITUDE n. *a tired, trite old saying; a banality*
Remember our bombastic mayor? Well, one reason he's so boring is that he just mouths *platitudes*, like all windbags, and everybody's tired of hearing the same old sayings. *Platitudes* put people to sleep.

MEMORY FIX
To learn these new words, write each one on a sheet of paper. Also write a synonym or definition for each and say the new words aloud as you work.

TRUE OR FALSE
Read each sentence below to see how each word in this chapter is being used. Then mark **T** (true) or **F** (false) beside each.

1. You wouldn't enjoy a *raconteur* at your party. _____

2. We have many *euphemisms* for the word "died." _____

3. Hugh's repertoire of *hackneyed* jokes makes us roar with laughter. _____

4. A *laconic* speech is sure to drag on forever. _____

5. If I ask for a *terse* report, I mean a *succinct* one. _____

6. We sat spellbound and attentive as the speaker uttered one *platitude* after another. _____

7. *Hyperbole* is often used to good effect in a *lampoon*. _____

8. A person with a fine mind probably created this *banal* essay. _____

9. A pompous, self-important person is apt to deliver a *bombastic* speech. _____

10. The more *articulate* you are, the greater our chance of understanding your message. _____

MATCHING
Match the words in column A with their meanings in column B.

	A	**B**
_____	1. eloquent	a. garrulous
_____	2. banality	b. great exaggeration
_____	3. vociferous	c. to say effectively
_____	4. trite	d. moving and expressive
_____	5. tautology	e. pompous
_____	6. articulate (v.)	f. evasive
_____	7. bombastic	g. platitude
_____	8. provoke	h. hackneyed
_____	9. loquacious	i. redundancy

_____ 10. laconic   j. sparing of speech

_____ 11. hyperbole   k. to arouse or spark

_____ 12. equivocal   l. insistent and loud

FILL IN THE BLANKS

From the words in this chapter, select the ones that best complete the meaning and logic of each sentence.

1. An editor who complains that your book lacks originality is saying that it is **t**_____ and **h**_____.

2. Five words that refer to the extremely economical use of language are **c**_____, **s**_____, **l**_____, **t**_____, and **p**_____.

3. "Mile-high pie" is an example of _____.

4. A **p**_____ is stale and overused, a trite remark, just like a **b**_____.

5. The opposite of a clearcut answer is a(n) _____ one.

Answers for this chapter begin on page 197.

SYCOPHANTS HAVE BROWN NOSES

despot • sycophant • glutton • hedonist • hypocrite • heretic • charlatan • bigot • miser • insurgent • zealot • skeptic

DESPOT n. *a ruler with total control; a tyrant, autocrat*
Dude, my five-pound Yorky, sees himself as king of our house, a real *despot* with all of us under his paw. Amy's cat, Meatloaf, never yields to doggy *despotism*, of course.

SYCOPHANT n. *a brownnoser; one who flatters others; a toady*
Kids dislike *sycophants* because their brownnosing is so hypocritical. Powerful people must enjoy that servile flattery or we wouldn't have so many *sycophants*.

GLUTTON n. *one who is overly, almost sinfully, hungry for something, usually food* n. **glut** v. **to glut**
Amy's a *glutton* for roles on stage. "I'll play any part," she says. Recently, wrapped in thick padding, she portrayed *Gluttony* itself in a Christian morality play about the seven deadly sins.

HEDONIST n. *someone who lives for pleasure or happiness*
In class we discussed the Greek's doctrine of *hedonism*, which held that happiness or pleasure was the sole good in life. We contrasted the *hedonist's* pleasure-seeking goals with the Putitan's spiritual, work-oriented life, and ended up voting for a blend of the two—the old Greek "golden mean."

HYPOCRITE n. *one who pretends to a life or beliefs that he doesn't honestly have; a phony or fake*
The guys I know don't admire a *hypocrite* or *hypocrisy* of any kind. It's so phony. Think about tennis star Arthur Ashe, who was always honest and straightforward, never phony. "Not a *hypocritical* bone in him," my friend Jason says.

ORA = to speak, pray

inexorable—*not movable by any means; inflexible, relentless*
inexorable hand of fate
the *inexorable* march of time

oracle—*one who gives wise or especially meaningful advice*
Greek *oracle* at Delphi
the principal, our school's *oracle*

Also: **oracular, orator, peroration** *(a long, grandiose speech)*

HERETIC n. *one who differs from accepted belief or theory*
"Would you guys hang me as a *heretic* if I suggested eliminating the Social Corner?" I asked the newspaper staff. They agreed to cut the column and admitted that occasionally *heretics* have good ideas. (But often the mere suspicion of *heresy* is fatal. Witches were burned as *heretics* by fanatics, remember?)

CHARLATAN n. *a quack or fraud; a cheat, imposter*
My dad's office is just recovering from being cheated by a master *charlatan* who posed as a management consultant. The real skill of *charlatans* is lying, apparently.

BIGOT n. *one who stubbornly holds to his own opinions*
I hope age doesn't turn me into a narrow-minded *bigot* like some I know. I hate prejudice, and *bigoted* people are usually very opinionated.

VER = truth

verify—*to establish truth or accuracy; to confirm*
verify his whereabouts
try to *verify* his statement

aver—*to state firmly and convincingly; declare positively*
"For all *averred*, I had killed the bird
That made the breeze to blow.
Ah wretch! said they, the bird to slay,
That made the breeze to blow!"
The Rime of the Ancient Mariner, Samuel Taylor Coleridge

Also: **verdict, verisimilitude, veracious** *(truthful)*

MISER n. *a greedy, grasping person (L. miser = miserable)*
One of my friends is really a *miser*, in contrast to the rest of us, who are mainly generous guys. We tease him about being a *miserly* Scrooge type, but his stinginess is less amusing as time goes by.

INSURGENT n. *a rebel; one who rises up in revolt*
As an editor I need to study newspapers, so I'm always aware of *insurgent* forces in other countries. My sympathies are with *insurgents* whenever they're revolting against a cruel political regime, as in Haiti.

ZEALOT n. *a fanatic; someone devoted beyond reason to a cause or belief*
As the self-appointed defender of the family, Dude is our personal *zealot*. Daily he patrols our property, barking *zealously*—fanatically—whenever a stranger threatens to cross over into his territory.

SKEPTIC n. *one who doubts or waits to pass judgment*
Thomas Huxley, the famous English biologist, knew that a good scientist was a *skeptic*. He said, "*Skepticism* is the highest of duties, blind faith the one unpardonable sin." A *skeptic* is the opposite of a zealot or fanatic.

MEMORY FIX
To learn these new words, write each one on a sheet of paper. Also write a synonym or definition for each and say the words aloud as you work.

FILL IN THE BLANKS
From the words in this chapter, select the one that best completes the meaning and logic of each phrase. Note which tense or form of the word is required for sense.

1. dangerous crew of armed _____ spearheading the revolt

2. the _____ habit of saying one thing while thinking another

3. needs one _____ week just having fun this summer

4. a true workaholic, a regular _____ for more challenges

5. as _____ as the cycle of the seasons

6. those practiced _____ who skillfully deceive us

7. looked like a real diamond, but I was still _____

8. a strong autocrat, but even so a benevolent

   _____

9. the _____ in our midst, determined to go against established tradition

10. suffering from an excess of zeal, a _____ for sure

11. hoarding his candy like a _____ hoards his wealth

12. the most _____, prejudiced person I ever met

13. the servile behavior of a known _____

14. necessary that you _____ the accuracy of this report

RHYME TIME

Complete these couplets of pretty awful poetry (PAP) with the correct form of one of this chapter's new words **or** an important synonym.

1. Said Orson Welles, whose size doubled by twice,

   "_____ is not a secret vice."

2. We keep loony Aunt Tilly up in the attic,

   'Cause everyone knows she's a raving _____.

3. When I need advice on a matter historical,

   I ask my teacher, the school's living _____.

4. A _____ says, "I was born to doubt,
   Until the facts of the matter come out."

5. We couldn't believe he gave her that plant,
   But he's a toady, you know, a _____.

6. "Lookin' for fun in all the right places,"
   Sings the _____ eager for bright party faces.

7. Nature's _____ laws we spurn,
   Only if we're too dimwitted to learn.

8. I was quick to _____ when I testified,
   That Hugo would never run off or hide.

MATCHING

In column B, find two synonyms or phrases to explain each word in
column A, and write their letters on the correct lines.

	A		**B**
_____	1. miser	a. bias	i. fake, fraud
_____	2. heretic	b. corroborate	j. one in revolt
_____	3. despot	c. hoarder	k. prejudice
_____	4. charlatan	d. nonbeliever	l. fanatical
_____	5. bigotry	e. rebel	m. Scrooge
_____	6. verify	f. tyrant	n. overeager
_____	7. zealous	g. imposter	o. confirm
_____	8. insurgent	h. autocrat	p. one who differs

Answers for this chapter begin on page 198.

HOW GERMANE, MY DEAR

---

fervent • germane • fortuitous • grueling • indulgent • vulnerable • profuse • superficial • uniform • listless • incessant • unobtrusive

---

FERVENT adj. *full of strong emotion; impassioned*
Meatloaf vents her anger in *fervent* yowls when another cat invades our yard. The *fervor* of Meatloaf's response to feline trespassers seems much louder at night, when we *fervently* wish she'd shut up.

GERMANE adj. *fitting and appropriate; relevant; pertinent*
The Mark Twain quotes I like best aren't *germane* to my talk, so I can't use them. Our speech teacher always says, "Omit the extras and concentrate on the *germane* material when giving a brief talk."

FORTUITOUS adj. *happening by chance; accidental*
Meatloaf stalks mice deliberately, but she also has her share of *fortuitous* meetings. Happening upon a mouse is *fortuitous* not only for Meatloaf but also for the mouse, who would never have planned to meet a cat.

GRUELING adj. *demanding and exhausting; punishing, tiring*
In one *grueling* day, the newspaper staff washed over 400 cars to raise money for a new computer. At home later, exhausted but proud, I told the folks just how *grueling* a task it had been.

INDULGENT adj. *generous to a fault; lenient, not critical*
We've been too *indulgent* with Dude, and so he's badly spoiled. We've agreed to stop *indulging* him right now. As Shakespeare warned us, an *indulgent* person loves "not wisely but too well."

VULNERABLE adj. *open to physical or mental damage or hurt*
Unaware of the word *vulnerable* as a kid, I still knew the feeling of being open to attack from mean guys on the playground at recess. When you're *vulnerable*, you know you're without a good defense.

CLAUS/CLUD/CLUS = close, shut

preclude—*to forestall, hinder, avert, or prevent*
    the storm *precluded* our hike
    that rule *precludes* his joining

recluse—*a hermit; one living a solitary life*
    a wealthy, eccentric *recluse*
    his withdrawn, *reclusive* life

Also: **exclude, exclusion, claustrophobia, include, inclusion**

PROFUSE adj. *in great abundance; bountiful; lavish; lush*
The phrase *"profuse* apologies" describes a gushing flood of "I'm sorrys." During a tough wrestling match, my *profuse* perspiration is another kind of flood. Unfortunately, our county has a *profusion* of great high school wrestlers.

SUPERFICIAL adj. *on the surface, shallow; not deep, serious, or important; cursory, not thorough*
I got some *superficial* cuts from cleats in the last soccer game; fortunately, *superficial* wounds normally heal without causing trouble. In contrast, a *superficial* judgment is apt to cause lots of trouble.

UNIFORM adj. *consistent (as opposed to varied); the same*
I think *uniformity* of design, as in a row of identical houses or apartments, is boring. But at school I want consistency and fairness—*uniform* attendance policies and *uniform* grading systems.

POT/POSS = to be powerful or able

potent—*powerful; effective or efficacious*
    a *potent* remedy
    a *potent* idea
    an Eastern *potentate* (ruler)

omnipotent—*all-powerful*
    omnipotent ruler
    the old Greek *omnipotent* gods

Also: **potential, possible, possess**

LISTLESS adj. *lacking energy or enthusiasm; indifferent or languid; uncaring*
When we found Meatloaf staring at her food with dull, *listless* eyes, we knew she was sick. Any *listlessness* toward dinner on that cat's part is serious. When I had the flu, I remember feeling *listless* toward everything.

INCESSANT adj. *going on without interruption; unceasing; continuous*
En route to the vet's office, Meatloaf's *incessant* yowling drove us bats. Like many cats in a car, she cries continuously and pitifully—an *incessant* reminder that she never asked to go for a ride.

UNOBTRUSIVE adj. *not noticeable; inconspicuous; or, not aggressive*
Our pets Dude and Meatloaf don't know the word *unobtrusive*. Meatloaf thinks, why utter a dainty, *unobtrusive* mew when you can yowl? And Dude has spent his entire aggressive life seeking fights instead of being *unobtrusive*.

MEMORY FIX
To learn these new words, write each one on a sheet of paper. Also write a synonym or definition for each and say the words aloud as you work.

FILL IN THE BLANKS
To complete each sentence, select the correct **noun form** (as shown below) of the adjectives in this chapter's list.

fervor	indulgence	listlessness	profusion
uniformity	superficiality	vulnerability	unobtrusiveness

1. I object to the _____ of this assessment, especially since I had requested an in-depth evaluation.

2. By the end of our vacation, I had relaxed to the point of almost total _____!

3. We were excited by the _____ of the cheering crowd that lined the marathon runners' path.

4. In Glacier National Park in late June, the wildflowers erupt on the hills and roadsides in brilliant _____.

5. Realizing the _____ of animals on our planet, concerned people have organized to protect these dependent creatures.

6. "I'm begging your _____ for a minute," the speaker said, "while I digress briefly."

7. From a human's viewpoint, the owl that sleeps by day and hunts silently by night is a model of _____.

8. When we bake chocolate chip cookies, we try for _____ so that all of them have the same amount of chocolate.

TRUE OR FALSE

Read each sentence below to see if the words in this chapter are being used properly. Then mark **T** (true) or **F** (false) beside each sentence.

1. If you've never really worked out at a health spa, the first experience is fun but a trifle *grueling*. _____

2. The painful twinges of out-of-shape muscles would be more acceptable if they were *incessant*. _____

3. His fondness for good company is only natural in a confirmed *recluse*. _____

4. Because his diving is still weak after years of practice, I think his *potential* is limited in that sport. _____

5. When a highway becomes treacherous, officials often *preclude* travel until conditions improve. _____

6. A pertinent anecdote is one that is *germane* to the topic.

   _____

7. The girl's *fervent* plea to the vet to save her beloved pet raccoon moved us to tears. _____

8. A planned, organized meeting cannot be termed *fortuitous*.

   _____

9. Erratic guidelines are more helpful than *uniform* ones. _____

10. An *unobtrusive* tooth fairy is the most successful. _____

MATCHING ANTONYMS

Knowing opposites is helpful. Match the words on the left by writing the letters of two antonyms on the correct lines.

_____ 1. germane	a. irrelevant	k. restful
_____ 2. profuse	b. weak	l. deeply serious
_____ 3. uniform	c. aggressive	m. inappropriate
_____ 4. grueling	d. restrained	n. stingy
_____ 5. superficial	e. inconsistent	o. unforgiving
_____ 6. potent	f. exhilarating	p. varied
_____ 7. indulgent	g. thorough	q. ineffective
_____ 8. listless	h. bouncy	r. friendly
_____ 9. reclusive	i. gregarious	s. enthusiastic
_____ 10. unobtrusive	j. critical	t. conspicuous

Answers for this chapter begin on page 198.

SNOOTS UP

---

arrogant • disdain • fastidious • haughty • disparage • deprecate • condescend • supercilious • contempt • pretentious • scoff • complacent

---

ARROGANT adj. *proud, overbearing; snootily self-important*
Despite his office, President Abraham Lincoln was never *arrogant*, but humble instead. A much later president, John F. Kennedy, said, "When power leads man toward *arrogance*, poetry reminds him of his limitations."

DISDAIN n. *scorn; snooty disapproval or dislike; contempt* v. **to disdain** adj. **disdainful**
No animal can show *disdain* as well as a cat. If Meatloaf's food is not quite right, she *disdains* to eat it and scratches around the bowl as if to bury the offending meal.

FASTIDIOUS adj. *extremely fussy and particular; meticulous*
A healthy cat is *fastidious* about its appearance and grooms its fur meticulously. A sick cat abandons this natural *fastidiousness*.

HAUGHTY adj. *openly and disdainfully proud; snooty* n. **hauteur, haughtiness**
You've heard that pride goes before a fall, but the old Biblical proverb actually says, "Pride goeth before destruction and a *haughty* spirit before a fall." You've seen *haughtiness*, that "I'm above you" attitude, right?

DISPARAGE v. *to belittle or downgrade (someone or something); to decry, depreciate, minimize*
When I was a kid, a bigger neighbor boy regularly *disparaged* my homemade tree house. I remember how that *disparagement* hurt and how it reduced my pride in my creation.

ROG = to ask

derogatory—*scornful, disparaging, downgrading, belittling*
    of a *derogatory* nature
    a highly *derogatory* critique

prerogative—*a special right or privilege*
    a ruler's *prerogative*
    her natural *prerogative* as the oldest

Also: **interrogate, arrogant, abrogate, surrogate**

DEPRECATE v. *to disapprove mildly, with regret* adj.
deprecatory, *hoping to avoid disapproval*
It's clear that Mom *deprecates* the mess in my room, but she understands that it's my space. When relatives are critical, Mom defends me with a *deprecatory* shrug and a smile.

CONDESCEND v. *to come down in level, unbend, stoop*
Meatloaf *condescends* to play hide-and-seek with Dude if she thinks no one will see her being kittenish again. Likewise, my serious, formal grandfather will now and then *condescend* to listen to my rock music.

SUPERCILIOUS adj. *excessively proud; disdainfully superior*
Explaining her role in our school play, Amy said, "I'm playing an insufferably snooty lady, someone totally *supercilious*. I'm supposed to reek of *superciliousness* in every speech.

RID/RIS = to laugh

deride—*to mock or make fun of; to ridicule*
    don't *deride* his shyness
    humbled by his *derision*

risible—*laughable, funny; used for laughter*
    a truly *risible* situation
    risible facial muscles

Also: **ridicule, ridiculous, risibility, derisive, derisory**

CONTEMPT n. *total lack of respect; disdain; scorn*
Our English class wrote essays on this Schopenhauer quote: "Hatred comes from the heart; *contempt* from the head; and neither feeling is quite within our control." That's probably true, but we can use *contempt* for good purposes, such as being openly *contemptuous* of those who damage our planet.

PRETENTIOUS adj. *showy, self-important, pompous; insisting on recognition, often unjustifiably*
The newly rich (nouveau riche, to my French teacher) often live in *pretentious* houses and drive expensive cars. *Pretentiousness* says, "Look at me. I'm important."

SCOFF v. *to make fun of, mock; to belittle by jeering or contemptuous talk*
A few times we *scoffed* at guys who got pinned in the first period of their wrestling matches, but the coach stopped that. "Come out to support each other, not to *scoff*," he ordered.

COMPLACENT adj. *self-satisfied, smug*
Dude quivers all over with *complacency* after chasing off an intruder. As he returns to his position on our porch, he twitches his topknot *complacently*—smug in the knowledge that he's done his duty.

MEMORY FIX
To learn these new words, write each one on a sheet of paper. Also write a synonym or definition for each and say the words aloud as you work.

MATCHING
Circle the two words or phrases that best explain the meaning of each of the words in bold type.

1. **fastidious**
   (A) swift
   (B) exceedingly particular
   (C) meticulous
   (D) unpleasant

2. **deprecate**
   (A) reduce
   (B) deny
   (C) disapprove of
   (D) regret

3. **arrogant**
   (A) prideful
   (B) questioning
   (C) thoughtless
   (D) overbearing

4. **condescend**
   (A) stoop
   (B) unbend
   (C) forgive
   (D) offend

5. **contempt**
   - (A) timely assistance
   - (B) scorn
   - (C) disdain
   - (D) refusal

6. **scoff**
   - (A) torture
   - (B) critique
   - (C) belittle
   - (D) mock or jeer

7. **complacent**
   - (A) smug
   - (B) self-satisfied
   - (C) peaceful
   - (D) well-located

8. **prerogative**
   - (A) annoyance
   - (B) privilege
   - (C) position
   - (D) right

9. **deride**
   - (A) scoff at
   - (B) dismount
   - (C) ridicule
   - (D) hoard

10. **disparage**
   - (A) resist
   - (B) minimize
   - (C) decry
   - (D) avoid

WORDS IN CONTEXT

Write the meaning of each italicized word on the lines provided.

1. back stiffly erect, nose *haughtily* in the air

   _____

2. filling an otherwise empty life with *pretentious* objects

   _____

3. raised a *supercilious* eyebrow and gave a loud "Humph!"

   _____

4. viewing the culprit with a look of utter *disdain*

   _____

5. gentle cleric who *disdained* pulp literature

   _____

6. cringing as he read the *derogatory* review

   _____

7. insulted by their *condescending* manner

_____

8. enjoying my *prerogative* as the leader

_____

9. bowing her head in a *self-deprecatory* way

_____

10. regarding my handiwork with a certain *complacence*

_____

ANALOGIES

Circle the one word pair in each list below that expresses the same relationship as the pair in capital letters.

1. **NAPOLEON : ARROGANCE**
   - (A) Ben Franklin : hedonism
   - (B) Hitler : fastidiousness
   - (C) Tchaikovsky : bombast
   - (D) Twain : satire
   - (E) Maya Angelou : journalism

2. **REMARK : DISPARAGING**
   - (A) appearance : unobtrusive
   - (B) attitude : scoffing
   - (C) speech : articulate
   - (D) article : meticulous
   - (E) design : risible

3. **PRIDE : HAUTEUR**
   - (A) pretentiousness : wealth
   - (B) disdain : disgust
   - (C) sorrow : contempt
   - (D) satisfaction : complacency
   - (E) youth : vulnerability

4. **DERISION : RIDICULE**
   - (A) sweetness : indulgence
   - (B) disdain : honor
   - (C) prerogative : duty
   - (D) seclusion : profusion
   - (E) scorn : contempt

Answers for this chapter begin on page 198.

LISTS 1–5 REVIEW

Here's one more chance to practice using the words in lists 1 to 5. But first, read each list and say each word and its meaning out loud. Over one third of us learn best through our EARS.

FIND THE ODDBALL

In each word group, cross out the oddball—the one *unrelated* word or phrase.

1. bigot   phony   hypocrite   heretic   fake

2. ridicule   derision   hauteur   disdain   derogation

3. insist   assent   comply   yield   acquiesce

4. clamorous   noisy   vociferous   persistently vocal   nasty

5. articulate   hyperbole   lucid   effective   clear

6. relevant   pertinent   germane   interesting   related to

7. provoke   preclude   forestall   hinder   prevent

8. proud   inevitable   arrogant   haughty   supercilious

9. flatterer   toady   sycophant   brownnoser   hedonist

10. hackneyed   terse   clipped   concise   succinct

TRUE OR FALSE

Check these sentences for correctness. Then mark **T** (true) or **F** (false) beside each.

1. *Euphemisms* allow you to say in public what would otherwise be unacceptable or possibly even cruel. _____

2. *Hackneyed* phrases, such as "he eats like a horse" or "she's thin as a rail," are not examples of *hyperbole*. _____

3. You should avoid hiring speakers who are very *eloquent*.

   _____

4. You shouldn't *verify* data for a research paper. _____

5. *Hedonists* are careful to avoid parties. _____

6. A *miser* enjoys supporting several charities. _____

7. *Zealots*, or *fanatics*, rarely *condone* ideologies that run counter to theirs and may even *disparage* contrasting views in a most *articulate* manner. _____

8. In *My Family and Other Animals*, Gerald Durrell pokes fun at everyone in his family, making a book-length *lampoon*. _____

9. As an ancient Greek general, you might wish to consult the famous *oracle* at Delphi before a battle. _____

10. If you prefer short meetings, select *loquacious* board members, not *laconic* ones. _____

FIND THE SYNONYM

From the choices offered, select the missing synonym for each numbered word group and write that synonym on the corresponding line.

> to concur   to condone   charlatan   profuse
> precursor   banal   inexorable   listless
> to chastise equivocal   grueling   potent

1. unclear evasive confusing undecided

_____

2. to agree coincide assent approve _____

3. trite hackneyed commonplace stale

_____

4. languid indifferent uncaring _____

5. to scold castigate punish censure _____

6. impostor quack fraud cheat _____

7. to overlook excuse pardon _____

8. forerunner harbinger herald _____

9. immovable relentless inflexible _____

10. punishing tiring demanding exhausting

_____

11. abundant bountiful lavish lush _____

12. powerful effective efficacious _____

WHO SAID THAT?

From the choices offered, write the *type of speaker* for each of the following comments.

raconteur   glutton   skeptic   interrogator
equivocator   heretic   recluse   orator
despot   insurgent   scoffer   deprecator

1. "Friends, Romans, countrymen, lend me your ears."

   _____

2. Did I tell you the one about Anansi the Spider and his cousin . . .? _____

3. Could I have another steak? _____

4. It's peaceful here alone on the island. _____

5. Are you sure? Did you run tests that prove your ideas are actual facts? _____

6. Clean your room now or else! _____

7. Gee, there's nothing like a good uprising. _____

8. That's nothing. I was riding a bike at age three.

   _____

9. I don't believe that anymore; I can't. _____

10. Well, maybe and maybe not. It sort of seems that way, and then again it doesn't. _____

11. I repeat. Is that your toad in the soup? _____

12. I didn't really mean to, she said, shrugging.

    _____

MATCHING

Match the words in column A with their meanings in column B and then write the meanings in the space provided.

		A	B
_____	1.	coalesce	pompous language
_____	2.	laud	accidental
_____	3.	cursory	to ridicule
_____	4.	bombast	disdain, scorn
_____	5.	platitude	to scatter or fan out
_____	6.	aver	to obliterate; wear away
_____	7.	fortuitous	lenient
_____	8.	deride	continuous
_____	9.	prerogative	to praise
_____	10.	contempt	superficial or hasty
_____	11.	augment	to come together
_____	12.	disperse	to declare firmly
_____	13.	efface	banality
_____	14.	indulgent	to increase
_____	15.	incessant	right or privilege

Answers for this review lesson begin on page 199.

VERBS TO HEED

---

garner • mar • heed • meander • nullify • obliterate • mitigate • obscure • peruse • raze • placate • rebuff

---

GARNER v. *to gather or collect; accumulate; earn*
Our paper's sports editor *garners* all the information he can about an opponent before a crucial game. He says, "I go to their practices with the goal of *garnering* any clue, however small, that will help us to compete better."

MAR v. *to spoil or damage; to injure or blemish*
We all hate having something nice *marred*. For instance, a zit really *mars* a kid's appearance. When flying gravel *marred* the paint on Dad's new car, he went ballistic.

HEED v. *to listen to, pay attention to, consider; to mind*
Meatloaf *heeds* our orders only if she feels like it. Deep in a cat's soul must be the motto: To *Heed* is To Yield Independence. One day, *heedless* of our pleading, Meatloaf made her way to the top of the neighbor's giant oak.

MEANDER v. *to wander casually with no set plan; to ramble*
A speech should not *meander* but should follow a clear outline; nor should an airplane *meander* through the skies. But I'm glad that streams and creeks *meander* in no set pattern across the countryside.

NULLIFY v. *to render unimportant or without worth; to negate or invalidate; to annul legally*
The Student Council voted to *nullify* some regulations passed by former councils. We made them *"null* and void," as the expression goes.

OBLITERATE v. *to erase completely, wiping out all traces*
A group of us watched from a high dune as the tide came in and *obliterated* our sand castles, leaving the shore flat and smooth. I wish I could *obliterate* as completely those old, childish nightmares.

MUT/MUTAT = to change

immutable—*changeless and unchanging; unalterable, eternal*
Nature's *immutable* laws
the *immutable* power of love

mutation—*significant genetic change; the one changed*
a *mutation* in the human form that evolved over time
scientifically engineered *mutations* in corn plants

Also: **mutable, mutant, commute, permutation, transmutation**

MITIGATE v. *to ease, making less severe; to alleviate or relieve*
We slathered antihistamine cream on Amy's bee stings, hoping to *mitigate* the pain. She said that the burning and itching were somewhat *mitigated* but certainly not obliterated.

OBSCURE v. *to make dim or unclear; to conceal, hide* adj.
obscure, *vague, mysterious, remote, dark*
As a wrestler, I like to *obscure* the real objective of my movements and catch an opponent off guard. Chess and checkers players *obscure* their strategies, too, I'm sure.

PERUSE v. *to study or examine carefully* n. **perusal**
The guidance counselors urged us to *peruse* the booklet *Taking the SAT*. Also, they suggested we *peruse* a self-help book that explains each kind of problem. After a *perusal* of *SAT Success*, I decided I needed to brush up on geometry.

PON/POS = to place or put

posit—*to suppose, propose, suggest; to assume or affirm*
let's *posit* this theory
when he first *posited* that idea

proponent—*one who talks in favor of something, an advocate*
a famous *proponent* of exercise
hardly a *proponent* of sloth

Also: **position, postpone, component, exponent, repository, expose, depose, transpose, deposit, dispose, juxtapose**

RAZE v. *to tear down completely, to demolish*
We spent last weekend *razing* the old barn on our property. We'd hoped to save it, but since it was too decrepit to restore, we were forced to *raze* it instead.

PLACATE v. *to calm, soothe, or appease, especially by offering to "be nice" or to do someone a favor*
Last year's seniors were a crazy bunch, always in trouble and trying to *placate* the principal for what they'd done. As time weny by, she said she couldn't be *placated* any longer.

REBUFF v. *to criticize harshly or to reject someone, often by snubbing them (ignoring them)*
Meatloaf *rebuffed* Dude's offers of puppy friendship when he first joined our family. Do you think a dog feels hurt the way a human does when he suffers a *rebuff?* Dude didn't allow himself to be *rebuffed* for long, of course.

MEMORY FIX

To learn these new words, write each one on a sheet of paper. Also write a synonym or definition for each and say the words aloud as you work.

RHYME TIME

Complete these couplets of pretty awful poetry with the correct form of one of the new words in this chapter.

1. An unusual word that at first makes us frown,

   To _____ a building means to tear it down!

2. Something _____ forever stays the same,
   Unlike that fleeting idol called fame.

3. The detective announced, "A theory I'll _____.
   The criminal's hiding right here in this closet."

4. Down fragrant paths of rose and oleander,
   My love and I were happy to _____.
   (Oh, brother.)

5. A _____ is a really odd star for a show,
   But remember those Ninja turtles we know?

MATCHING

Circle the two words or phrases that best explain the meaning of each of the words in bold type.

1. mar
   (A) blemish
   (B) confuse
   (C) spoil
   (D) annoy

2. mitigate
   (A) discuss
   (B) adjust
   (C) relieve
   (D) alleviate

3. obliterate
   (A) disguise
   (B) efface
   (C) wipe out
   (D) cover up

4. rebuff
   (A) snub
   (B) restore
   (C) polish
   (D) reject

5. garner
   (A) avoid
   (B) collect
   (C) strew around
   (D) accumulate

6. obscure
   (A) cloud over
   (B) conceal
   (C) caution
   (D) negate

7. peruse
   (A) scan
   (B) memorize
   (C) study carefully
   (D) examine

8. meander
   (A) walk
   (B) wander
   (C) ramble
   (D) flirt

9. placate
   (A) enjoy
   (B) entertain
   (C) soothe
   (D) appease

10. raze
   (A) lift up
   (B) tear down
   (C) devour
   (D) demolish

11. nullify
   (A) invalidate
   (B) join legally
   (C) end
   (D) negate

12. heed
   (A) wait on
   (B) mind or obey
   (C) consider
   (D) learn

SUBSTITUTION

Replace each italicized word or phrase with the correct word from the word list in this unit, including words from roots.

1. I refuse to *pay attention to* that wacko advice!

    _____

2. She's always been a *person in favor* of recycling. _____

3. That splash of aftershave certainly *spoiled* the tabletop.

    _____

4. The digressive nature of his lecture unfortunately *made dim, mysterious, and unclear* his major points. _____

5. Her explanation should *soothe and relieve* Claire's anger.

    _____

6. Queen Elizabeth I *firmly rejected* those who even hinted that the English Navy might lose to the Spanish Armada.

    _____

7. We were finally able to *make promises of never doing that again* Mom and Dad, but it wasn't easy. _____

8. I spent hours *studying carefully* the driver's manual before I took the test. _____

9. As long as they adhere to the Constitution, members of the Supreme Court may *render null and void* a decision by a lower court. _____

10. At summer meets with neighboring towns, Amy has *collected* several awards for backstroke and freestyle swimming.

    _____

Answers for this chapter begin on page 200.

BEWARE A PARSIMONIOUS PREDECESSOR

---

virtuoso • termerity • volition • torpor • quandary • trepidation • zenith • reticence • respite • parsimony • nostalgia • predecessor

---

VIRTUOSO n. *a highly skilled performer*
As Meatloaf yowled eloquently from the top of the oak tree, Dad observed, "Hmm, we have a true feline *virtuoso*. Now if only she were a *virtuoso* at climbing, she could get herself down from there."

TEMERITY n. *unwise boldness; rash or reckless behavior*
Meatloaf showed unusual *temerity* in scaling that oak. Dude, of course, is forever hurtling into danger with a *temerity* that would never occur to a more sensible dog.

VOLITION n. *use of your own will, by your choice*
Animals were once viewed as beings of instinct only, with no powers of *volition*. Now we know that animals act on their own *volition* fairly often.

TORPOR n. *sluggishness, lethargy; inability to think or act quickly* adj. **torpid**
To be absolutely pooped is to feel *torpor*. I was in a totally *torpid* state once after a grueling wrestling match. Boxers must feel a similar *torpor* after their matches.

QUANDARY n. *a feeling a puzzlement or doubt*
Choosing a college is a perplexing process that has most of us in a state of *quandary*. It's a *quandary* that will remain, I think, until the final decision is made.

TREPIDATION n. *fear, worry, apprehension*
I keep seeing the phrase "in fear and *trepidation*," which seems repetitious, because *trepidation* often means fear. I'd rather say, "He went forward timidly, with *trepidation*."

ARCH = chief or main; ruler

hierarchy—*a series arranged by rank or grade*
>   at the top of the *hierarchy*
>   her place in the *hierarchy*

anarchy—*lack of government, often resulting in lawlessness*
>   historical *anarchy* in the Balkans
>   *anarchy* in the ranks

Also: **patriarch, matriarch, monarch, archangel, architect**

ZENITH n. *the highest point, or acme; point of culmination*
Although *zenith* means the highest point in the sky above us, I more often hear it used in phrases like "when his powers were at their *zenith*" or "at the *zenith* of her career."

RETICENCE n. *quietness and restraint in personality* adj. **reticent**, *silent, restrained, reserved*
President Calvin Coolidge, a silent, restrained New Englander, was famous for his *reticence*. On hearing that this most *reticent* of men had died, writer Dorothy Parker said, "How can you tell?"

RESPITE n. *time of relief from activity; rest, pause, lull*
Thanksgiving weekend came as a welcome *respite* after a crazy autumn. That's the purpose of a vacation, of course—to act as a *respite* from our normal, busy lives.

LU/LUC = light

lucid—*clear and distinct; sensible, intelligible*
>   a graceful, *lucid* talk
>   having recovered *lucid* speech

elucidate—*to explain fully and clearly*
>   *elucidate* his problem, please
>   always happy to *elucidate*

Also: **lucidity, translucent, luminous, Lucifer, lucubration**

PARSIMONY n. *extreme stinginess; thrift; penny-pinching*
As all of Dickens's readers know, the character Ebenezer Scrooge is synonymous with *parsimony*. Underpaying his staff and failing to heat his business office were only a few of Scrooge's *parsimonious* habits.

NOSTALGIA n. *a sentimental longing for a past time or state*
adj. **nostalgic**
My grandparents are a typically *nostalgic* pair who always tell the same stories about my dad as a kid. *Nostalgia* for the past and the way things were must be a natural part of growing older.

PREDECESSOR n. *an ancestor; prior person in a position*
My *predecessor* on the newspaper was an editor who turned the various staff members into a close family of coworkers. My grandparents, who are my hereditary *predecessors* and who aren't one bit parsimonious, generously provide a vacation spot for our entire family each summer.

MEMORY FIX
To learn these new words, write each one on a sheet of paper. Also write a synonym or definition for each and say the words aloud as you work.

FILL IN THE BLANKS
From the new words in this chapter, select the one that best completes the meaning and logic of each sentence. Note which tense or form of the word is required for sense.

1. Meadowlark Lemon, a magician on the basketball court, and Itzhak Perlman, a gifted violinist, are both _____ in their respective fields.

2. The alternatives were so different and so complex that I was left in a complete _____.

3. When the anaesthetic has worn off and the patient is _____, the newspaper reporter will want to interview him.

4. A _____ man, Jacob Grunch amassed a fortune through careful management and total disregard of others' needs.

5. I wouldn't mind crossing the desert at night, but never when the sun is at its _____!

6. _____ in every limb of his body, the hibernating
   bear stretched slowly, then settled back into sleep.

7. I remember my summers at camp with _____,
   sorry that I'm too old to return.

8. Before the principal called him to her office, my friend Greg went
   of his own _____, hoping to mitigate her anger
   by his voluntary appearance.

9. Today's politicians don't dare be _____ folk,
   because the TV era demands articulate speakers.

10. We're amazed every year at the _____ of the
    squirrels who collect acorns from our porch, despite the vigilance
    of Meatloaf and Dude.

MATCHING ANTONYMS

Knowing opposites is helpful. Match the words on the left with their
opposites on the right.

_____	1. trepidation*	to obscure
_____	2. reticence	descendant
_____	3. zenith	hyperactive
_____	4. torpid	order
_____	5. temerity	confidence
_____	6. elucidate	beginner
_____	7. anarchy	generosity
_____	8. virtuoso	nadir (lowest point)
_____	9. predecessor	bombast
_____	10. parsimony	timidity

* Knowing what trepidation is, what does *intrepid* probably mean?

_____

FIND THE ODDBALL

In each word group below, cross out the oddball, the one unrelated word or phrase.

1. ranking   hierarchy   assortment   series

2. break   angle   rest   lull   respite

3. niece   ancestor   grandparent   predecessor

4. instinct   will   volition   desire

5. apprehension   worry   temperament   trepidation

6. quest   preplexity   quandary   puzzlement

7. betrayal   stinginess   miserliness   parsimony

8. transparent   coherent   intelligible   lucid

9. rashness   fear   boldness   temerity

10. quaintness   restraint   silence   reticence

Answers for this chapter begin on page 200.

THAT'S ME!

---

astute • discerning • formidable • indefatigable • sage • profound • judicious • meticulous • painstaking • resilient • tenacious • benevolent

---

ASTUTE adj. *wise, shrewd, perceptive; perspicacious*
Like everyone in my class, I hope to make a fairly *astute* college selection. Luckily, our guidance counselors are pros and have made several *astute* suggestions that will help me to narrow my choices.

DISCERNING adj. *showing wisdom and wise judgment; discriminating wisely among choices* v. **to discern** n. **discernment**
Emily Dickinson wrote, "Much Madness is divinest Sense—To a *discerning* eye." My class wrote short essays on that couplet, trying to *discern* its meaning. We're gradually becoming *discerning* readers and interpreters of poetry.

FORMIDABLE adj. *fostering respect or awe; arousing fear; redoubtable*
Because the opponents I'd normally face in our next wrestling meet are *formidable* beyond belief, I have to sweat down to the next lowest weight class in order to wrestle competitively. Of course, nothing helps a guy sweat like the fear of a *formidable* adversary!

INDEFATIGABLE adj. *untiring, tireless (see root of "fatigue")*
Mom's *indefatigable* determination to learn computer programming is amazing. Our whole family is stubborn, though, so the word *indefatigable* often applies to us.

SAGE adj. *wise as a result of experience and thought; shrewd and discerning of judgment; prudent* adj. **sagacious, shrewd** n. **sage**, *wise elder*
Look at all the meaning *sage* conveys in only four letters. Perhaps author Ernest Hemingway made a very *sage* decision by using mostly short, punchy words.

LEV = light (as in weight), to raise

leverage—*a form of control, power, or effectiveness; referring to the use of a lever*
> used his position as *leverage* in the takeover

alleviate—*to lessen or relieve the severity of a condition*
> *alleviate* his pain
> hoping to *alleviate* their sorrow

Also: **elevate, levitate, elevator, lever, levee, levity**

PROFOUND adj. *intellectually deep; deeply important; complete or all-encompassing*

Our new principal is a *profoundly* thoughtful man, given to uttering *profound* thoughts whenever they occur to him. This talkativeness is a *profound* change from his predecessor, who was extremely reticent.

JUDICIOUS adj. *showing good judgment; wise, discreet*

I always think of *judge*, *justice*, and *jury* when I see the root *ju*, an old root of Jove and Zeus that actually means "shining sky." Of course, gods have always been thought to live in the sky and to be the most *judicious* of beings.

METICULOUS adj. *particular down to the tiniest detail*

Meatloaf is a *meticulous* groomer. This care results in a glossy fur coat that advertises her *meticulous* nature.

TEN/TENT/TIN/TAIN = to hold, contain

tenet—*a major belief, principle, or doctrine of a group*
> a main *tenet* of Judaism
> one *tenet* of that profession

untenable—*indefensible; unable to be occupied (by a tenant)*
> a wholly *untenable* theory
> a rundown, *untenable* building

Also: **tenant, tenure, content, contention, detain, detention, contain, abstain, abstinence, sustain, sustenance**

PAINSTAKING adj. *revealing much care and effort*
With *painstaking* care, I restored the used car that I inherited on my eighteenth birthday. In the true sense of the word *painstaking*, I took great pains to wash, paint, and wax every inch of this incredible treasure.

RESILIENT adj. *elastic; able to "snap back" after change or misfortune* n. **resilience**
Dude's personality is *resilient*; he bounces back to his cheerful, optimistic self within minutes of being scolded. Without this natural *resilience*, he'd be sorrowful much of the time, because he gets frequently corrected.

TENACIOUS adj. *persistent in holding on (as "barnacles are tenacious"); retentive (as "a tenacious mind")* n. **tenacity**, *courage*
If I had a more *tenacious* mind, I'd be able to remember history dates and math formulas better. Luckily, I'm a pretty *tenacious* wrestler—a real bulldog.

BENEVOLENT adj. *showing good will (Also from bene = good are benefactor, benign, beneficent, etc.)*
In world history we studied Charlemagne, an educated and *benevolent* French king who ruled for the good of his people. We debated the virtues of a *benevolent* dictatorship in class.

MEMORY FIX
To learn these new words, write each one on a sheet of paper. Also write a synonym or definition for each and say the words aloud as you work.

FIND THE SYNONYM
From the choices offered below, select the missing synonym for each word group and write it in the space provided.

astute	resilient	tenacious	alleviate	tenet
profound	formidable	meticulous	untenable	

1. awesome   inspiring fear   redoubtable _____

2. deeply intellectual   all-encompassing _____

3. indefensible   unable to be inhabited _____

4. belief   dogma   principle   doctrine _____

5. able to spring back to form   elastic _____

6. perceptive   shrewd   wise   perspicacious _____

7. extremely careful   attentive to detail _____

8. persistent   determined   retentive _____

9. relieve   lessen   lighten   reduce _____

TRUE OR FALSE

Read each sentence to see if it makes sense. Then mark **T** (true) or **F** (false) beside each.

1. Every bit of homework requires *indefatigable* effort. _____

2. By definition, a *benefactor* is usually *benevolent*. _____

3. Being *meticulous* about your appearance for a job interview is probably a waste of time. _____

4. If you insert the end of a stout board beneath that boulder, you'll have the *leverage* needed to move the rock. _____

5. The cult leader's insistence that he was Jesus Christ put him in an *untenable* position. _____

6. No one bothers to try to *alleviate* the symptoms of poison ivy.

_____

7. Typically, *painstaking* folks are among the most prized in hospital operating rooms. _____

8. Rarely can you arrive at a *judicious* decision in seconds. _____

9. If you have to have a tumor, let's hope it's *benign*. _____

10. *Discerning* which chocolate chip cookies should win the blue ribbon would be a disgusting job. _____

11. The last quality you'd want in a fight is *tenacity*. _____

ANALOGIES

Circle the one word pair in each list below that expresses the same relationship as the pair in capital letters.

1. **LAWYER : ASTUTE**
   (A) artist : insightful
   (B) chemist : beneficent
   (C) pathologist : painstaking
   (D) instructor : resilient
   (E) detective : awe-inspiring

2. **PROFOUND : THOUGHTFUL**
   (A) meticulous : painstaking
   (B) judicious : discreet
   (C) shrewd : astute
   (D) sagacious : bright
   (E) fearful : terrified

3. **SUPREME COURT : SAGACITY**
   (A) swimmer : tenacity
   (B) bones : tension
   (C) symphony : benevolence
   (D) muscles : resilience
   (E) city council : tenure

4. **FORMIDABLE : DEFENSE**
   (A) indefatigable : enemy
   (B) perspicacious : tenant
   (C) judicious : friend
   (D) discernible : traitor
   (E) redoubtable : warrior

Answers for this chapter begin on page 200.

PAIRS OF POPULAR OPPOSITES

---

abstract/concrete • **lax/stringent** • **atrophy/burgeon** • **affluent/indigent** • **cacophony/euphony** • **optimism/ pessimism** • **gravity/levity** • **desecrate/consecrate** • **resolute/irresolute** • **objective/subjective** • **refutable/ irrefutable**

ABSTRACT adj. *indefinite; vague; theoretical; intangible*
CONCRETE adj. *definite or specific; real, tangible*
When I watch our team captain wrestle, I'm seeing a *concrete* display of courage, which is itself an *abstract* concept. Friendship is another *abstraction*, but my friends are real, *concrete* human beings.

LAX adj. *loose; unstructured; not firm; negligent; slack*
STRINGENT adj. *tight or constricted; rigid, adhering firmly to accepted standards*
At orientation for new counselors, the camp director handed us a *stringent* set of rules for the camp. "If rules are dangerously *lax*," he said, "we have a dangerous camp."

ATROPHY v. *to wither, degenerate; to waste away*
BURGEON v. *to flourish; to grow and quickly expand; bloom*
Ideas *burgeon* in people's minds just as flowers or weeds *burgeon* in soil. By contrast, anything that *atrophies* is faring poorly, like muscles that *atrophy* from illness.

AFFLUENT adj. *wealthy in a material sense*
INDIGENT adj. *very poor; lacking necessary material goods*
A guest lecturer at our school spoke on the contrast between Haiti's few *affluent* people and all the others—people so *indigent* that they live on the hills in three-sided shacks.

PHON = sound

phonics—*a system of sounds for letters, groups of letters, and syllables; acoustics, the science of sound*
>   learned *phonics* early in school
>   a new *phonics* system

symphony—*harmonious musical composition; symphony orchestra*
>   beauty of a Beethoven *symphony*
>   the Boston *Symphony*

Also: **telephone, sousaphone, phonetics, phonograph, euphony, cacophony**

CACOPHONY n. *displeasing, harsh sound; horrible noise*
EUPHONY n. *pleasing or sweet sound; harmony (of speech)*
Parents and kids have different ideas about *euphonious* sound. Our folks often call our music *cacophony* when it is absolute *euphony* to us. Any judgment about *cacophony* versus *euphony* seems pretty subjective.

OPTIMISM n. *a positive, upbeat, favorable outlook on life*
PESSIMISM n. *a negative, discouraging outlook on life*
For Mark Twain, Tom Sawyer represented *optimism*. Huck Finn, who was a stark realist, embodied *pessimism*. Comics joke that a *pessimist* is a person who has all the facts. An *optimist*, of course, focuses on the encouraging facts.

SACR/SECR/SANC = sacred, holy

sacrilege—*the desecration (profaning) of something holy*
>   the inescapable *sacrilege* of war
>   his swearing, a *sacrilege*

sanctity—*holiness, sacredness*
>   the *sanctity* of the church
>   for the *sanctity* of her soul

Also: **sacrosanct, inner sanctum, sacred, consecrate, desecrate**

GRAVITY n. *weighty importance; seriousness*
LEVITY n. *lightness of approach or treatment; humor*
We probably should treat the SATs with *gravity*, as the results can make a big difference in our lives. But I'm not just a number, and my score doesn't say who I am. My friends and I joke about SATs a lot, because *levity* helps us get past tough challenges.

DESECRATE v. *to defile or profane something sacred or very special*
CONSECRATE v. *to make sacred or holy or worthy of respect; to hallow*
Most Americans don't want anyone to *desecrate* our flag, our national anthem, or our monuments—anything that has special, emotional significance to us. Those things have been *consecrated* over time in our culture.

RESOLUTE adj. *firmly determined; steady; faithful*
IRRESOLUTE adj. *uncertain about behavior; vacillating*
I acted in a totally *resolute* manner last Halloween when I took some neighbor kids through a famous "haunted house." If I'd seemed nervous or *irresolute* for even a second, those kids would have bolted like spooked horses.

OBJECTIVE adj. *lacking personal feeling or involvement; in a detached, unbiased, fair manner*
SUBJECTIVE adj. *colored by personal feeling or opinion*
All kids wish that the grading of writing were more *objective* than it is; unfortunately, *subjective* factors always creep in. Our English teachers mark one grade on papers for the *objective* items like grammar, with a separate grade for creativity, which is a more *subjective* judgment.

REFUTABLE adj. *shaky in foundation, therefore able to be refuted (proved wrong or false)*
IRREFUTABLE adj. *impossible to refute (prove wrong or false)*
My lawyer cousin said he's only interested in *irrefutable* evidence that can't be disproved in court. *Refutabe* evidence is clearly worthless.

MEMORY FIX
To learn these new words, write each one on a sheet of paper. Also write a synonym or definition for each and say the words aloud as you work.

WORD ANALYSIS

Fill in the blanks in the sentences below based on this chapter's word list.

1. Euphonious sound makes you feel _____, contrasted with cacophony, which is _____.

2. The _____ sees the glass as half full; the _____ sees it as half empty.

3. Psychologists say that somewhat _____, dependable rules provide children the necessary "fences" needed for security, whereas _____, unstable guidelines undermine their security.

4. _____ judgments are unclouded by emotion, whereas _____ judgments reflect the feelings of the judge.

5. A poem is a _____ thing; poetry itself, an _____ idea.

6. We speak of plants as things that _____ and grow, then eventually wither. Ideas or muscles that waste away or wither are said to _____ from lack of use.

7. The _____ '80s saw people busily acquiring luxuries, not just the necessities of life, which _____ people lack.

8. Humor provides the _____ that enables us to survive the _____ of situations beyond our control.

9. We _____ the senior medallion in the entryway of our school with a solemn ceremony. Any underclassman who _____ it will be dead meat.

10. Mom's _____ skill with homemade brownies was proved at the last bake sale. Now, if she says we don't need her brownies at a bake sale, that notion will be easily

   _____.

11. The Cowardly Lion was a timid, _____ fellow in the Oz books, but as soon as he had courage he behaved in a most _____ manner, full of determination.

USING THE WORDS

Write the new words from this chapter on the correct lines below.

1. to wither away = _____
   to flourish, bloom = _____

2. can't be proved wrong = _____
   apt to be disproved = _____

3. impersonal = _____
   colored by feeling = _____

4. to profane = _____
   to hallow = _____

5. vague, indefinite = _____
   definite, real = _____

6. loose, lenient = _____
   tight, rigid = _____

7. horrible noise = _____
   pleasing sound = _____

8. rosy outlook = _____
   negative outlook = _____

9. seriousness = _____

   lightness, humor = _____

10. firmly determined = _____

    unsure, vacillating = _____

Answers for this chapter begin on page 201.

THE BLUES

---

irascible • writhe • taciturn • tawdry • servile • surreptitious • rancor • sullen • remorse • rue • malice • malign

---

IRASCIBLE adj. *easily angered; testy, choleric, touchy*
Irascible after her bath at the vet's, Meatloaf snarled at Dude and me and then hid under the sofa. Poor Meatloaf. She's usually a pussycat, not an *irascible* grouch.

WRITHE v. *to twist; twist sideways in pain or suffering*
Writhing from side to side is the natural movement of snakes like the Southwestern sidewinder. When people *writhe*, they are either suffering pain or perhaps dancing. I've done a bit of *writhing* myself, on the wrestling mat.

TACITURN adj. *naturally silent, untalkative; laconic*
A *taciturn* person would enjoy this George Eliot quote: "Blessed be the person who has nothing to say who refrains from giving wordy evidence to that fact."

TAWDRY adj. *cheap-looking; showy, gaudy* n. **tawdry**, *showy, cheap finery*
Tawdry is a bit of British history that became a word. St. Audrey's laces were wispy silk necklaces sold for the saint's feast day. The words St. Audrey were run together, and '*taudrey's* laces were actually cheap and showy, so a new word gradually evolved.

SERVILE adj. *subservient, abject, annoyingly submissive*
Amy's latest role cast her as a *servile* maid who is always whining, "Anythin' more, yer lordship?" I dislike that *servile*, cringing attitude because it seems hypocritical.

SURREPTITIOUS adj. *secretive, deceptive; clandestine*
Does everybody take *surreptitious* little bites of cookie dough? Or *surreptitious* peeks at letters not addressed to them?

MON/MONIT = warn, advise, remind

admonish—*to warn strongly, reprove; show disapproval*
she *admonished* the kittens not to lose their mittens

premonition—*forewarning or foreboding; presentiment*
a *premonition* of disaster
troubled by *premonitions*

Also: **admonition, monitor, remonstrate, monument**

RANCOR n. *deep-seated bitterness; old enmity*
I've seen this cliché several times: "He viewed his old foe with *rancor*," and I know from experience that *rancor* is a bitter feeling.

SULLEN adj. *quietly resentful; lowering; gloomy, dismal*
For an understanding of the word *sullen*, it's hard to beat Robert Burns's lines in *Tam o'Shanter*: "Whare sits our sulky, *sullen* dame, Gathering her brows like gathering storm, Nursing her wrath to keep it warm."

REMORSE adj. *self-reproach, regret; a guilty uneasiness*
I feel some *remorse* if I squash a ladybug, because they're harmless, but I never regret flattening a wasp or bumblebee. I doubt that a wasp feels *remorse* when it stings me.

RUE v. *to regret exceedingly; feel remorse or sorrow*
Gramma is always saying I'll "*rue* the day" I became a car owner, and the poet A. E. Housman warned that giving your heart to a girl results in "endless *rue*." If I believe them, I'll be regretting something all my life!

MEDI = middle

mediate—*to reconcile by acting as an intermediary or go-between in a dispute*
happy to *mediate* for both sides
involved in *mediation*

medicore—*of only ordinary quality or low quality*
unfortunately *mediocre* performance
only *mediocre* at best

Also: **mediator, intermediate, medium, medieval**

MALICE n. *the desire to see another suffer; extreme ill will or spite* adj. **malicious**
A disillusioned Mark Twain wrote in his *Autobiography*: "Of the entire brood, he [man] is the only one—the solitary one—that possesses *malice*. That is the basest of all instincts, passions, vices—the most hateful . . . He is the only creature that inflicts pain for sport, knowing it to *be* pain. . . ."

MALIGN n. *to slander, defame; speak of in an ill-willed manner*
Although we've published critical profiles in the school paper, we've never actually *maligned* anyone's character. Tabloids thrive on *maligning* famous people, but our staff regards that as yellow journalism.

MEMORY FIX
To learn these new words, write each one on a sheet of paper. Also write a synonym or definition for each and say the words aloud as you work.

FILL IN THE BLANKS
From the new words and roots in this chapter, select the one that best fits the meaning and logic of each phrase.

1. an _____, demanding boss who quickly lost her temper

2. still brooded on it years later, consumed by _____

3. an uneasy _____ that something would go wrong

4. reading the book _____ under the covers at night

5. reduced a touching story to a cheap, _____ thriller

6. gave us a cheerful, forgiving look, not a _____ one

7. _____ on the sidewalk in pain after spraining an ankle

8. working at replacing with charity the _____ he once felt

9. a naturally withdrawn, _____ personality who feels little need for talk

10. wearing the typical _____ look of a sycophant or toady

11. spoken with cruelty and _____, meant to be hurtful

12. to feel strong regret or remorse is to _____ something

MATCHING

For each word in column A, find two synonymous words or phrases in column B and write their letters on the appropriate lines at the left.

	A	**B**	
_____	1. remorse	a. slander	k. forewarning
_____		b. laconic	l. quietly resentful
_____	2. premonition	c. bitterness	m. guilty unease
_____		d. cheap	n. defame
_____	3. malign	e. secretive	o. deceptive
_____		f. foreboding	p. lowering
_____	4. sullen	g. subservient	q. silent
_____		h. self-reproach	r. choleric
_____	5. rancor	i. testy	s. gaudy
_____		j. abject	t. old enmity
_____	6. tawdry		
_____			
_____	7. surreptitious		
_____			
_____	8. taciturn		
_____			
_____	9. servile		
_____			
_____	10. irascible		
_____			

RHYME TIME

Complete these couplets of pretty awful poetry* with the correct form of one of the new words in this chapter.

1. It's me and Jane Fonda, lean and lithe,
But some days this twist is a painful _____.

2. Regretful, sorrowful, sorry Sue,
Hers is a heart laden with _____.

3. Children are _____ in Mother Goose rhyme,
To be careful, watch out, and be home on time.

4. Nasty and mean was witchy old Alice,
Her mind just brimmed with spite and _____.

5. Folks whose mental skills are _____
Should perhaps think twice before playing poker.

6. To _____ is to resolve a dispute,
By compromise, not by acting cute.

Answers for this chapter begin on page 201.

---

* Okay, *terrible* poetry.

LISTS 6–10 REVIEW

Reviewing is the best way to keep these words forever. First, reread lists 6–10, saying each word aloud. You, too, may be someone who learns best through your ears.

FIND THE SYNONYM

From the choices offered below, find the missing synonym for each word group and write it in the space provided.

obsecure	immutable	mitigate	burgeon
lucid	respite	abstract	taciturn
astute	parsimonious	sacrilege	resolute

1. dark vague mysterious remote _____

2. alleviate ease relieve lessen _____

3. unchanging eternal unalterable _____

4. break rest pause lull _____

5. stingy penny-pinching miserly _____

6. distinct clear sensible intelligible _____

7. perspicacious shrewd wise perceptive _____

8. indefinite theoretical intangible _____

9. flourish grow blossom bloom _____

10. determined faithful steady _____

11. desecration fouling profaning _____

12. laconic silent untalkative reticent _____

ANALOGIES

Circle the one word pair in each list below that expresses the same relationship as the pair in capital letters.

1. **SYMPHONY : VIOLINS**
   (A) admonition : manager
   (B) council : agenda
   (C) choir : music

   (D) religion : tenet
   (E) jury : oath

2. **ENERGY : TORPOR**
   (A) holiness : consecration
   (B) government : anarchy
   (C) phonics : speech

   (D) thought : discernment
   (E) heaviness : gravity

3. **SIN : REMORSEFUL**
   (A) shack : tawdry
   (B) mistake : rueful
   (C) carelessness : marred

   (D) problem : refuted
   (E) error : hopeful

4. **PAST : NOSTALGIA**
   (A) time : abstraction
   (B) sun : zenith
   (C) present : pessimism

   (D) philosophy : perusal
   (E) future : optimism

5. **MEDIATE : SAGE**
   (A) placate : sister
   (B) meander : guide
   (C) elucidate : teacher

   (D) posit : parent
   (E) refute : director

6. **BATTLE : TREPIDATION**
   (A) acquaintance : levity
   (B) general : hierarchy
   (C) enemy : rancor

   (D) dispute : gravity
   (E) sorrow : reticence

MATCHING ANTONYMS

Knowing opposites is helpful. Match the words in column A with their antonyms in column B.

	A	**B**
_____	1. predecessor	lax
_____	2. affluent	malicious
_____	3. gravity	scan
_____	4. stringent	ignore
_____	5. resilience	heir
_____	6. benevolent	temerity
_____	7. placate	indigent
_____	8. peruse	silly
_____	9. heed	irritate
_____	10. judiciousness	levity
_____	11. profound	even-tempered
_____	12. irascible	rigidity

FILL IN THE BLANKS

From the choices offered below, select the word that best completes the meaning and logic of each sentence. Be sure to put each word into the correct grammatical form.

volition	tenacious	raze	obliterate
garner	reticent	virtuoso	quandary
rebuff	irrefutable	meticulous	proponent zenith

1. A glance at Amy's trophies and you'd think her whole goal in life was to _____ swimming awards.

2. Even after several months, I'm still as _____ about the upkeep of my old used car as I was at first.

3. My friend Juan is _____ on every topic but music, the one subject that really loosens his tongue.

4. I wish that females understood how afraid guys are of being
_____ when they call girls for dates.

5. A wrecking crew _____ the old theater and
carted away all the debris, thus _____ all traces
of the structure.

6. In Dicken's *A Tale of Two Cities*, Sydney Carton goes to the
gallows of his own _____ in order to save
another man's life and thereby secure a woman's happiness.

7. Our neighbors were in a _____ over what to call
their new French restaurant until Dad suggested "Le Snail."

8. "Well, Meatloaf," Mom said accusingly, "these feathered corpses
are _____ evidence of what you did last night!"

9. Martin Luther King was one of the most eloquent
_____ of equality of opportunity for all Americans.

10. To study tennis _____, look at some old clips of
Arthur Ashe, Martina Navratilova, and John McEnroe.

11. As one who remembers everything she's read, my Aunt Jolly must
have one of the world's most _____ minds.

12. Michael Jackson reached the _____ of his career
at a very young age compared with most performers.

Answers for this review lesson begin on page 202.

VACILLATE NOT!

---

acclaim • rejuvenate • revere • sanction • temper •
saturate • whet • scrutinize • vacillate • thwart •
venerate • waive

ACCLAIM v. *to proclaim or announce with noisy approval,
such as shouts and applause* n. **acclaim** and **acclamation**
The first time he was in a dog show, Dude found the *acclaim* he loves.
When he was *acclaimed* as Best of Breed in the Yorkshire terrier class,
he strutted in front of the audience with obvious delight in their
applause.

REJUVENATE v. *to make youthful or like new again; to renew
or reinvigorate*
The restoration of my old secondhand car has *rejuvenated* it entirely.
"You've accomplished a total *rejuvenation*," Dad told me, gazing at it
with admiration.

REVERE v. *to respect and honor; to venerate, worship* n.
reverence
For the Puritans, the words *revere, respect,* and *venerate* described
much of their lives. They taught their children to *revere* God, their
country, adults, and one another.

SANCTION v. *to confirm, authorize; endorse, approve, support*
n. **sanction**, *authorization, approval* n. **sanctions**, *forceful
measures to assure compliance with law (usu. international)*
Although Senior Skip Day is an old tradition, our principal has said, "I
can't *sanction* it, although I'll probably condone it again. Obviously, no
principal can *sanction* the breaking of school rules."

TEMPER v. *to moderate or adjust as conditions require; or, to
strengthen through hardship*
In his inaugural address, John F. Kennedy referred to Americans as a
people "*tempered* by war, disciplined by a hard and bitter peace." Thirty
years later, we are trying to *temper* our military needs and attend to
other urgent problems.

CLAM/CLAIM = to shout, cry out

clamor—*great outcry or shouting; noisy or confused demand*
the *clamor* of his fans
all *clamoring* for attention

disclaim—*to deny or disavow; speak in denial; repudiate*
disclaim all knowledge
file a *disclaimer* (legal denial)

Also: **acclaim, exclamation, exclaim, proclaim, proclamation, declaim, declamation, reclaim, reclamation**

SATURATE v. *to fill completely; satiate, soak*
If I study in Spain for a college semester, I can *saturate* myself with Spanish. The best way to learn any language is by total immersion or *saturation*.

WHET v. *to excite or stimulate (the mind or appetite); to hone or sharpen (a knife or mind)*
In *Sea Fever*, poet John Masefield wrote, "I must down to the seas again, to the vagrant gypsy life, To the gull's way and the whale's way, where the wind's like a *whetted* knife." Great old poems like that *whet* everyone's appetite for more.

SCRUTINIZE v. *to examine minutely, with close attention* n. scrutiny, *close examination*
Now that Dude's in dog shows occasionally, we've learned to *scrutinize* him from head to tail before judging. He seems to enjoy being *scrutinized*, probably because he's so vain.

PLEX/PLIC/PLY = to fold

imply—*to suggest or hint without stating directly*
implied I ought to diet
stung by her *implication*

explicit—*fully and precisely revealed; without question*
follow her *explicit* orders
a need for you to be *explicit*

Also: **complex, complicate, comply, implication, explicate, reply, replicate, replica**

VACILLATE v. *to fluctuate; to change from one opinion to another; also, to hesitate*
"People who *vacillate* drive me right up the wall," Dad says. "I work better with definite, confident people, not folks who are *vacillating* like a bunch of dithering birds!"

THWART v. *to foil, baffle, or frustrate (someone's attempts)*
A young Yorky named Princess has pranced onto the show dog scene and may *thwart* Dude's chances for Best of Breed next year. Having been *thwarted* myself in wrestling matches, I know how tough it is to come in second-best.

VENERATE v. *to revere, respect, and admire with deference* adj. venerable, *worthy of respect*
No matter how he acted, King Henry VIII of Britain expected his subjects to *venerate* him. Today's royal family, to the open dismay of the *venerable* Elizabeth II, is forfeiting its right to *veneration* by behavior no longer overlooked.

WAIVE v. *to give up voluntarily; relinquish; forgo or postpone*
An obviously guilty student *waived* his right to a trial in student court. My family has a home court, but no one ever yields without being heard; we're all too independent to *waive* a chance at justifying our actions.

MEMORY FIX
To learn these new words, write each one on a sheet of paper. Also write a synonym or definition for each and say the words aloud as you work.

SUBSTITUTION
Replace each italicized word or phrase with the correct word from the list of words in this chapter, including words from roots.

1. "Fresh paint and wallpaper will absolutely *make like new again* this old apartment," Mom told our elderly aunt.

   _____

2. "Quit *shilly-shallying* and dive in," the swim coach yelled.

   _____

3. "Are you *hinting* that I dye my hair?" Aunt Jolly teased as she patted her bright red-orange curls. _____

4. Consideration for others' feelings sometimes causes us to *adjust as conditions demand* honesty with thoughtfulness.

   _____

5. After her astonishing victory in the relay, Amy was greeted with *noisy shouts of approval.* _____

6. Confucius taught his followers to *respect and honor* their elders.

   _____

7. Mom and Amy *carefully examined* the menu before ordering giant taco salads. _____

8. "I absolutely *refuse to acknowledge* any dog this muddy," Mom said, grinning at filthy little Dude. _____

9. A recent class debate focused on the *legal restrictions* against whaling in U.S. waters, because we can no longer *endorse or authorize* killing those endangered mammals.

   _____

10. A brief explanation of the case showed us why the defendant had *relinquished* his right to a trial by jury. _____

FIND THE ODDBALL

In each word group, cross out the oddball, the one unrelated word or phrase.

1. fill up   satiate   sponge   soak   saturate

2. twist   sharpen   excite   stimulate   whet

3. thwart   flinch   frustrate   foil   baffle

4. dankness   clamor   outcry   shouting   uproar

5. implied   fully revealed   precise   explicit   unquestionable

6. defer to venerate honor deter revere

7. urge support authorize endorse sanction

8. repudiate deny discourage disavow disclaim

9. forgo yield willingly relinquish relegate waive

10. reject inspect scrutinize examine study carefully

TRUE OR FALSE

Read each sentence to see how the words in this chapter are being used. Then mark **T** (true) or **F** (false) beside each sentence.

1. Medication doesn't need to come with *explicit* advice. _____

2. You should *thwart* the baby's attempt to ride a tricycle down the porch steps. _____

3. It's great when your idea meets with universal *acclaim*. _____

4. Just as steel is *tempered* for strength, so are survival skills *tempered* during hard times. _____

5. Exciting previews *whet* our desire to see a movie. _____

6. Sleeping people appreciate a soothing *clamor* nearby. _____

7. Avoid being *saturated* with knowledge before exams. _____

8. You can't *rejuvenate* road pizza. _____

Answers for this chapter begin on page 202.

HOW MUCH IS A DEARTH?

---

brevity • criterion • delineate • ephemeral • copious • dearth • evanescent • paucity • prodigious • meager • redundant • scanty

---

BREVITY n. *shortness, briefness; conciseness of expression*
In *Hamlet* our class found this famous quotation: "*Brevity* is the soul of wit." And in Coleridge's poetry we found: "What is an Epigram? a dwarfish whole, Its body *brevity* and wit its soul." Coleridge and Shakespeare probably would have laughed at the same short jokes.

CRITERION n. *a standard used for making judgments* pl. **criteria**
After all the basic *criteria* for judging dogs have been satisfied, a judge looks for a happy, friendly dog. For pet owners, temperament is always the most important *criterion* for evaluating a dog.

DELINEATE v. *to portray accurately; outline, describe*
The guidance counselor *delineated* the various aspects of college applications. She concentrated most on the essays, with a careful *delineation* of the criteria for a good essay.

EPHEMERAL adj. *short-lived, fleeting, transient*
It's good that mosquitoes, gnats, and flies have *ephemeral* lives. But my time in high school is beginning to seem pretty *ephemeral* too, and that's not so good.

COPIOUS adj. *superabundant; in plentiful supply*
Our yard has a *copious* supply of moles, which are awfully destructive. We're waiting for Meatloaf-the-Assassin to turn that *copious* number into a dearth.

MIN = less, little

minuscule—*very, very small*
   a *minuscule* insect
   a pitiful, *minuscule* effort

mince—*to chop very fine; to walk or talk in an affected way*
   mince the onions
   she *minced* her way down the aisle

Also: **minus, diminish, diminution, minority, miniature**

DEARTH n. *scarcity or lack; paucity*
Our class debated the poet Keats's comment on "the inhuman *dearth* of noble natures" and disagreed with Keats. "There's no *dearth* of good people," our teacher said, "but it's the other kind who make headlines."

EVANESCENT adj. *fading or vanishing quickly, like vapor; transient* n. **evanescence**
Ghosts are naturally *evanescent*, or so the story goes. I was a Halloween trick-or-treat ghost years ago, but a guy under a sheet isn't nearly as *evanescent* as he'd like to be.

PAUCITY n. *lack or scarcity of number or amount*
The word *paucity* is rarely used, except on SATs or PSATs. I often read about the "lack of" something or that "only a few exist," but for standardized tests, *paucity* lives on. Sigh.

MAGN = great, large

magnanimous—*generously forgiving; big-spirited*
   a *magnanimous* gesture
   the *magnanimous* nature of his soul

magnate—*someone of power, rank, or influence*
   an oil *magnate*
   the current banking *magnate*

Also: **magnify, magnificent, magnitude, magnanimity**

PRODIGIOUS adj. *inspiring awe; enormous in size or capacity*
Dinosaurs were creatures of *prodigious* size and exotic appearance, two qualities that fascinate. Children especially have a *prodigious* appetite for facts about dinosaurs.

MEAGER adj. *lacking in quality or quantity; scanty, skimpy, spare, sparse* also, **meagre**
I have used *meager* to describe tons of things. For instance: a narrow house on a *meager* lot; an old woman, *meager* of frame and stooped; he made only a *meager* effort; and why did you give me such a *meager* amount of spaghetti when I'm starving?

REDUNDANT adj. *extra and unnecessary; superfluous; unneeded* n. **redundancy**
Redundancies are tautological expressions that drive editors nuts. For example, "young kitten" and "young foal" are *redundant* because kitten and foal refer only to animals that are young. Also, "first and foremost" is a *redundant* expression.

SCANTY adj. *brief or short; lacking desired amount or size; meager*
I thought I liked *scanty* swimsuits until I saw my girlfriend in the *scantiest* bikini on earth. I instantly became Mister Jealous Boyfriend and said she couldn't wear that *scanty* excuse for a suit where anyone else could see her.

MEMORY FIX
To learn these new words, write each one on a sheet of paper. Also write a synonym or definition for each and say the words aloud as you work.

FILL IN THE BLANKS
From the new words in this chapter, select the one that best completes the meaning and logic of each sentence. Use the correct form of the word.

1. In order to choose a winner fairly, all contestants must be judged on the same _____.

2. Please _____ which topics to cover in this essay.

3. Will there ever be a day when there's a _____ of problems and a _____ supply of good answers?

4. Amy _____ across the stage, self-conscious from head to toe.

5. An affluent newspaper _____ funds ten scholarships.

MATCHING

Circle the two words or phrases that best explain the meaning of each word in bold type.

1. **brevity**
   (A) description
   (B) briefness
   (C) humor
   (D) conciseness

2. **delineate**
   (A) draw freehand
   (B) show artistically
   (C) outline
   (D) portray accurately

3. **prodigious**
   (A) wasteful
   (B) immense
   (C) enormous
   (D) liberal

4. **dearth**
   (A) scarcity
   (B) ground
   (C) paucity
   (D) soil

5. **ephemeral**
   (A) fleeting
   (B) transient
   (C) beautiful
   (D) sorrowful

6. **meager**
   (A) narrow-minded
   (B) Tarzan growl
   (C) scanty
   (D) skimpy

7. **redundant**
   (A) clamorous
   (B) unnecessary
   (C) dimwitted
   (D) superfluous

8. **magnanimous**
   (A) generous in spirit
   (B) large rodent
   (C) uncomfortably large
   (D) big-hearted

WORDS IN CONTEXT

Write the meaning of each italicized word on the lines provided.

1. certainly the most important *criterion* for acceptance

   _____

2. wealthy oil *magnate* from the Middle East

   _____

3. the *evanescent* fragrance of perfume

   _____

4. a list of *copious* complaints

   _____

5. only a *minuscule* amount of whipped cream

   _____

6. shouldn't *mince* words with her

   _____

7. enjoyed the depth and *brevity* of his talk

   _____

8. King Arthur's legendary *magnanimous* nature

   _____

9. numerous *redundant* sentences to be cut

   _____

10. renovation demanded a *prodigious* amount of energy

    _____

MATCHING ANTONYMS

In the column on the right, find two antonyms for each word at the left.

_____	1. ephemeral	copious
_____		scanty
_____	2. copious	meager
_____		tiny
_____	3. scanty	abundant
_____		superabundance
_____	4. dearth	plentiful amount
_____		enduring
_____	5. prodigious	minuscule
_____		long-lived

Answers for this chapter begin on page 203.

AN ECLECTIC COLLECTION

---

aesthetic • eclectic • gratuitous • inevitable • irony •
expedient • apocryphal • heinous • mundane •
arduous • prodigal • quixotic

AESTHETIC adj. *referring to a sense of beauty; artistic*
Poet James Terry White recognized the importance of *aesthetic* needs, recommending that you "buy hyacinths to feed thy soul." Flowers are *aesthetically* necessary to some; others, like me, need music or time alone in a wilderness area.

ECLECTIC adj. *carefully selected from many good sources*
I have a small but *eclectic* assortment of tapes and CDs ranging from the Dead to Tchaikovsky. Amy says our house is furnished in an *eclectic* manner, but our stuff is really just a collection of hand-me-downs from a large family.

GRATUITOUS adj. *offered freely, but not necessary under the circumstances, therefore unwanted or unneeded*
I guess everyone with a big family has one relative known for *gratuitous* advice. Ours is Uncle Mort, who drops his *gratuitous* comments into every conversation.

INEVITABLE adj. *unavoidable*
Uncle Mort's steady string of helpful advice used to annoy me, but now I know it's *inevitable*. His verbal wind is just as *inevitable* as the wind outside.

IRONY n. *the opposite of what would be normal or expected; humor based on incongruity* adj. **ironic**
Mom says that the real *irony* about Uncle Mort is that he's so often right. Most *ironic* of all is his habit of being right about kids, although he has none himself.

LEG/LECT/LIG = to choose, pick, read

predilection—*natural preference; positive feelings for*
    cat's *predilection* for mice
    her *predilection* for jazz

negligible—*of only minor importance, if any*
    a *negligible* difference
    his influence was *negligible*

Also: **legion, legation, legible, illegible, legumes (beans and peas that are picked), eligible, select, legacy**

EXPEDIENT adj. *suitable, practical, or advisable; also, opportunistic* n. **expediency**
In history class we discussed the view that the bomb dropped on Hiroshima was an *expedient* action undertaken to end World War II. Many felt that *expediency* had obscured morality in that case, so we had a heated argument.

APOCRYPHAL adj. *of doubtful authorship; fictitious*
Highly visible or controversial people often have comments attributed to them that are *apocryphal*. Even so, *apocryphal* quotations have a habit of surviving.

HEINOUS adj. *shockingly awful, appalling; abominable, outrageous*
Cult leaders Jim Jones and David Koresh led their followers into death, thereby committing a *heinous* crime: murder. Mass murder of trusting people is as *heinous* as anything I can imagine.

LEG = law

legitimate—*correct by law; conforming to accepted procedure*
    a *legitimate* driver
    a logical, *legitimate* reason

legislate—*to formally enact as law; to rule legally*
    a recently *legislated* statute
    our state *legislature*

Also: **legal, illegal, legitimize, legate** *(official emissary)*

MUNDANE adj. *everyday, commonplace, like menial chores*
As the opposite of celestial or heavenly, anything *mundane* should be dull, but it isn't always. Washing the car is a *mundane* chore, but I like slopping around on a wet driveway.

ARDUOUS adj. *demanding, hard to achieve; strenuous*
Packing gear into a wilderness camping area seems *arduous* to some, but not to me and my friends. For my friend Rob, writing an essay is an *arduous* job.

PRODIGAL adj. *wildly extravagant or lavish in spending*
Mom and Dad don't talk about our government's *prodigal* spending; they yell. They feel strongly about using funds wisely, so none of us is *prodigal* with money.

QUIXOTIC adj. *extravagantly idealistic; unpredictable; unrealistic or imaginary*
The word *quixotic* comes from the character Don Quixote in Cervantes's novel, a story of a lovable, wacky old fellow who imagines that he's a knight. *Quixotic* ideas are strange, a little crazy, but often wonderful.

MEMORY FIX
To learn these new words, write each one on a sheet of paper. Also write a synonym or definition for each and say the words aloud as you work.

MATCHING
Match the words in column A with their meanings in column B and write the meanings in the spaces provided.

	A	B
_____	1. gratuitous	opportunistic
_____	2. inevitable	insanely idealistic
_____	3. expedient	abominable, appalling
_____	4. arduous	commonplace
_____	5. quixotic	unwanted or unneeded
_____	6. apocryphal	strenuous
_____	7. mundane	unavoidable
_____	8. heinous	of doubtful authorship

FILL IN THE BLANKS

From the words below, select the one that best completes the meaning and logic of this essay.

aesthetic   ironic   predilection   negligible
eclectic   prodigal   legislate   legitimate

Meatloaf's undisguised _____ for small, furry critters results in many "gifts" left on the porch for our family. Last year's presents from Meatloaf were a(n) _____ array of mice, moles, birds, and shrews. In the summer, Meatloaf was absolutely _____ with these offerings, which we found pretty gross as time went on.

There's no _____ reason for her to hunt." Mom fumed. "We feed her enough that she could ignore her cat instincts!" Both Mom and Amy wish we could _____ a cat's behavior, but cats adhere strictly to their own laws.

"No point in scolding. Anything you say to a cat has only a _____ effect on its behavior," Dad observed. "How _____ that we should love a hunter," he went on, "when we're such fervent pacifists."

Of course, the grace and beauty of cats appeal to the _____ senses of many people, not just to our family.

ANALOGIES

Circle the one word pair in each list below that expresses the same relationship as the pair in capital letters.

1. **DAYDREAMING : QUIXOTIC**
   - (A) bicycling : expedient
   - (B) giving : prodigal
   - (C) reading : legitimate
   - (D) cleaning house : mundane
   - (E) eating : aesthetic

2. **BAD : HEINOUS**
   - (A) gratuitous : free
   - (B) aesthetic : artistic
   - (C) prodigal : scanty
   - (D) proposed : legitimate
   - (E) difficult : arduous

3. **APOCRYPHAL : LEGEND**
   - (A) long-range : goal
   - (B) fictitious : fable
   - (C) inevitable : story
   - (D) gratuitous : gossip
   - (E) hero : prodigal

FIND THE ANTONYM

Pair the words below with their antonyms by writing them on the correct lines.

parsimonious	haphazard	significant	apocryphal
aversion	quixotic	customary	mundane
noble	desired	avoidable	impractical

_____ 1. authentic

_____ 3. inevitable

_____ 4. gratuitous

_____ 5. negligible

_____ 6. predeliction

_____ 7. eclectic

_____ 8. heinous

_____ 9. ironic

_____ 10. heavenly

_____ 11. prodigal

_____ 12. expedient

Answers for this chapter begin on page 203.

YAKKETY YAK

---

verbose • blasphemy • vilify • diatribe • vitriolic • jargon • satire • tirade • slander • garble • rhetoric • garrulous

---

VERBOSE adj. *using more words than necessary; wordy*
When the teacher writes *VERBOSE!* across the top of my paper, I know I got carried away with descriptions again. The sin of *verbosity* is shared by many writers, of course, Stephen King included.

BLASPHEMY n. *disrespect or irreverence toward something sacred or seriously important* n. **blaspheme**
Playwright George Bernard Shaw wrote in *Pygmalion,* "Independence? That's middle-class *blasphemy*. We are all dependent on one another, every soul of us on earth." And later he said, "All great truths begin as *blasphemies*."

VILIFY v. *to slander or defame someone's name or standing in the community; to malign* n. **vilification**
The tabloid papers you see in the grocery store will apparently *vilify* anyone in public life. Their *vilifications* of prominent figures make me shake my head and wonder.

DIATRIBE n. *bitter, critical speech or writing*
Diatribes flourish in politics, where people seem eager to criticize others. Negative, name-calling speeches were banned in our school elections so that anything resembling a *diatribe* was cut short.

VITRIOLIC adj. *burning or corrosive like acid; caustic*
Political activists sometimes give *vitriolic* speeches when they're trying to make a point. But hearing these emotional, *vitriolic* attacks usually turns me against the speaker.

QUER/QUIR/QUIS = to ask, seek

querulous—*complaining, fault-finding, fretful; petulant*
a *querulous* tone of voice
her repeated, *querulous* comments

inquisitive—*inquiring, questioning, curious*
an *inquisitive* mind
an *inquisitive* sort of person

Also: **acquire, acquisition, query, inquire, require, inquisition, perquisite (perk), exquisite, requisition, requisite**

JARGON n. *special language or terminology; dialect or hybrid language*
Every industry or specialty develops its own *jargon*—words and expressions that only the insiders know. Kids often develop a *jargon* that sets them apart from their parents.

SATIRE n. *comedy using laughter as a weapon to evoke a feeling of scorn along with amusement*
My history class is reading *Huckleberry Finn*, Twain's *satire* that ridicules the prejudice, stupidity, and hypocrisy in America in the mid-nineteenth century. Twain's insightful *satiric* pen gives us laughter along with truth.

TIRADE n. *a lengthy, emotional, critical speech*
Coaches tend to lapse into a *tirade* when a team player makes a serious mistake. For those who have to listen to them, *tirades* are extremely memorable.

DIC/DICT = to speak, say; words

indict—*to charge with an offense, in court or informally*
indicted for the crime of murder
indicted by my own family

edict—*a formal order or command; a command by law*
Mom's *edict* on bedtime
the governor's latest *edict*

Also: **dictate, predict, indicate, indicative, dictatorial, dictionary, dictaphone, dictator, predicate**

SLANDER n. *a false, defamatory spoken criticism of someone* v. *to defame with untrue speech*
While libel can be either written or oral, *slander* refers to nasty, personal criticism that is oral only. Both *slander* and libel can be grounds for a lawsuit.

GARBLE n. *to change or alter meaning through misrepresentation of facts or distortion of ideas*
If you want to *garble* a message, just play telephone as you did at kids' birthday parties. One *garbled* message I remember began as "Who's Superman?" and ended up "Where's Pooh's can?"

RHETORIC n. *insincere or high-flown writing or speech; originally, the study of good communication*
Rhetoric has degenerated from something admirable and worthy of study to something contemptible, as when we accuse someone of "mere *rhetoric*." A *rhetorical* question is one asked for effect, with little hope of a serious answer.

GARRULOUS adj. *extremely talkative, gabby, loquacious, verbose* n. **garrulity**
Our Aunt Jolly is pretty *garrulous*, but we enjoy her verbosity because it's funny and never cruel. *Garrulity* turns people off if it drones on in a negative, critical way.

MEMORY FIX
Again, to learn these new words, write each one on a sheet of paper. Also write a synonym or definition for each and say the words aloud as you work.

SUBSTITUTION
Replace each italicized word or phrase with the correct word from the list of words in this chapter, including words from roots.

1. The teacher explained the assignment by asking several *just-for-effect* questions to get us thinking. _____

2. Don't *badly interpret* that information, please.

_____

3. His talk wasn't a lecture, it was a *bitter, critical speech* on the evils of drinking. _____

4. Jonathan Swift's most biting *comedy arousing scorn* was "A Modest Proposal," in which he suggested a grisly solution to the Irish famine. _____

5. "Have some dessert?" shrieked Amy. "When you know I'm dieting? That's an *unthinkable insult or disrespect*!"

_____

6. Gabbing throughout dinner and the movie is one sure way to get yourself described as *extremely talkative*. _____

7. It's taking Mom and Dad a while to learn the *special language* that goes with computers. _____

8. After hearing the evidence, the jury *formally charged* the suspect on a charge of grand larceny. _____

9. As we watched the movie, I felt my youngest cousin grow tense during the evil Queen's *lengthy, emotional speech* against innocent Snow White. _____

10. Respectable newspapers are careful not to print *material that would damage someone's reputation*. _____

TRUE OR FALSE

Read each sentence to see if it is correct. Then mark **T** (true) or **F** (false) beside each.

1. If you want folks to think you're a rocket scientist, you'll need a bit of rocketry *jargon*. _____

2. If people in the audience say, "Hmm, more *rhetoric*," at the end of your speech, you'll feel proud. _____

3. When you're asking Dad if you can borrow the car, a *vitriolic* tone will probably work the best. _____

4. Swearing is unacceptable *blasphemy* to many people. _____

5. The cartoon strip *Doonesbury* uses *satire* to good advantage. _____

6. A *querulous* "Why aren't you up?" starts the day right. _____

7. Truly vicious *slander* can *vilify* a person almost beyond redemption. _____

MATCHING

From the column on the right, select two synonyms or phrases that explain each of the words at the left and write in your answers.

_____	1. verbose	corrosive
_____		petulant
_____	2. vilify	wordy
_____		questioning
_____	3. querulous	defame
_____		legal order
_____	4. vitriolic	command
_____		malign
_____	5. edict	slander
_____		caustic
_____	6. inquisitive	curious
_____		garrulous
_____	7. slander	dishonor
_____		fretful

Answers for this chapter begin on page 204.

WISHY-WASHY

---

ambiguous • capitulate • defer • ambivalence •
dubious • languor • fluctuate • tentative • indifferent •
lethargy • innocuous • stagnant

AMBIGUOUS adj. *indefinite, open to more than one interpretation; obscure, uncertain* n. **ambiguity**
When Mom asked if the snake was loose in the house, I gave an *ambiguous* reply to keep her from worrying. But Mom hates *ambiguity*, and she said, "Yes or no? Be definite!"

CAPITULATE v. *to give in, surrender, acquiesce*
I *capitulated* under pressure and admitted that the snake was somewhere in the house. I begged Mom to stay in her room until we'd found him, and she *capitulated* readily.

DEFER v. *to yield to someone of greater authority or age; to put off until another time* n. **deference**
After finding the snake wrapped around the warm coils of the refrigerator, we *deferred* to Mom's wishes and moved him to the garage. I can no longer *defer* making him a stout cage.

AMBIVALENCE n. *fluctuation between one thing and another; uncertainty or indecision*
People are rarely *ambivalent* about snakes; either they like them or not. Mom hasn't any *ambivalence* about them whatever and thinks they all belong in zoos.

DUBIOUS adj. *doubtful; of questionable truth or quality; suspicious*
Unfortunately, Mom regards my fondness for wildlife as a *dubious* character trait. When I adopted a box turtle, she said he was of *dubious* value as a pet.

VAD/VAS = to go

evade—*to avoid, dodge, or circumvent a person or issue*
  evaded the issue
  evaded detection
  her *evasive* answer

pervade—*to go throughout, to diffuse throughout, to permeate*
  hint of fear *pervaded* the room
  a *pervasive* odor of skunk

Also: **evasion, invade, invasion, pervasion**

LANGUOR n. *sluggishness; tiredness or weakness; lethargy* adj. **languid**

Cats are *languorous* animals, stretching and yawning sleepily in the sun, then flopping down to doze again. This *languor* is true of cats of all types; cats sleep more hours a day than most other animals.

FLUCTUATE v. *to shift up and down; or, to come and go, as ocean waves*

Newscasters report daily *fluctuations* in the stock market, in temperatures, and in public opinion on current topics. Emotions *fluctuate* too, of course, according to what's happening in our lives.

TENTATIVE adj. *hesitant, unsure, uncertain*

E. B. White, author of *Charlotte's Web* and coauthor of *The Elements of Style*, warns us about *tentative* writing. "Vigorous writing is concise," he says, "and definite." Prose hedged with qualifiers is not only *tentative*, of course, it's also more wordy.

DUC/DUCT = to lead, direct

deduce—*to conclude or infer by reasoned thought*
  deduce that from the evidence
  a clever *deduction*

conducive—*apt to promote or assist*
  atmosphere *conducive* to learning
  a bed *conducive* to rest

Also: **induce, induction, reduce, reduction, seduce, seduction, conduct, conduction, abduct, deduct**

INDIFFERENT adj. *not good or bad; unconcerned or not curious; aloof or detached; unbiased*
An *indifferent* student doesn't care about learning. Someone who regards flowers with an *indifferent* eye isn't interested in flowers. *Indifference* can extend all the way to total detachment.

LETHARGY n. *serious tiredness; languor, laziness, torpor*
The *lethargy* of cats is rooted in their physiological need for sleep because of hearts and lungs proportionately smaller than those of other animals. When on a chase, though, the *lethargic* cheetah is the fastest critter on land.

INNOCUOUS adj. *harmless; or, dull, insipid*
The school's play director said he was tired of doing safe, *innocuous* plays. This year's play may cause a few raised eyebrows, but it certainly isn't *innocuous*.

STAGNANT adj. *unmoving or not flowing (stagnant water); stale (stagnant air); inactive* v. **stagnate**
We've all seen *stagnant* ponds and met people who have let their minds *stagnate*. A new word was born about twenty years ago when *stagnation* married *inflation* and created *stagflation*, an economic term describing stubborn inflation blended with *stagnant* consumer demand and noticeable unemployment.

MEMORY FIX
And again . . . hang in there and write each new word and a synonym or definition for each. Say the words aloud as you write them.

WORDS IN CONTEXT
Write the meaning of each italicized word based on how it is used in its quotation.

1. George Bernard Shaw: "The worst sin towards our fellow creatures is not to hate them, but to be *indifferent* to them: that's the essence of inhumanity." _____

2. Samuel Johnson: "I will be conquered; I will not *capitulate*."

   _____

3. Francis Bacon: "*Defer* not charities till death." _____

4. President Grover Cleveland: "After an existence of nearly 20 years of almost *innocuous* desuetude [disuse] these laws are brought forth." _____

5. Percy Bysshe Shelley, "To A Skylark":
"With thy clear keen joyance
Languor cannot be." _____

6. William Wordsworth, "National Independence and Liberty":
"Milton! thou shouldst be living at this hour:
England hath need of thee; she is a fen
Of *stagnant* waters." _____

7. Sir Isaac Newton, ". . . whatever is not *deduced* from the phenomena is to be called an hypothesis." _____

MATCHING
Circle the two words or phrases that best explain the meaning of each word in bold type.

1. **fluctuate**
   - (A) vary up or down
   - (B) group together in a flock
   - (C) disturb
   - (D) come and go

2. **dubious**
   - (A) old musical refrain
   - (B) suspicious
   - (C) of doubtful quality
   - (D) sneaky

3. **ambivalence**
   - (A) versatility
   - (B) medical vehicle
   - (C) wishy-washiness
   - (D) indecision

4. **tentative**
   - (A) hesitant
   - (B) unsure
   - (C) camping term
   - (D) timely

5. **lethargic**
   - (A) revolting
   - (B) languorous
   - (C) sick
   - (D) torpid

6. **ambiguous**
   - (A) two-faced
   - (B) enlarged
   - (C) indefinite
   - (D) uncertain

7. evade
  (A) avoid
  (B) hide
  (C) circumvent
  (D) fool

8. conducive
  (A) rewarding
  (B) promoting
  (C) punishing
  (D) assisting

9. pervade
  (A) become weird
  (B) dole out
  (C) permeate
  (D) diffuse thr oughout

FIND THE SYNONYM

From the choices offered below, select the missing synonym for each word group and write it in the space provided.

capitulate   stagnant   defer   innocuous
languor   tentative   evade   indifferent

1. dodge   avoid   circumvent   be elusive _____

2. yield in respect   postpone   suspend   put off

_____

3. sluggishness   weariness   torpor   lethargy _____

4. dull   harmless   insipid   inoffensive _____

5. stale   motionless   inactive   not flowing _____

6. unconcerned   detached   not curious   aloof

_____

7. hesitant   undeveloped   unsure   uncertain

_____

8. give in   yield   acquiesce   surrender _____

Answers for this chapter begin on page 204.

LISTS 11–15 REVIEW

Quick, quick, a handy review before those new words have a
chance to slip away. To begin, read over lists 11 to 15.
Say each word and its meaning aloud.

ANALOGIES

Circle the one word pair in each list below that expresses the same
relationship as the pair in capital letters.

1. **VACILLATE : AMBIVALENCE**
   - (A) disclaim : legitimacy
   - (B) whet : garrulity
   - (C) blaspheme : irreverence
   - (D) delineate : truth
   - (E) indict : suspect

2. **EPHEMERAL : DURATION**
   - (A) scanty : apparel
   - (B) negligible : interest
   - (C) inevitable : weather
   - (D) meager : amount
   - (E) minuscule : portion

3. **SATIRE : IRONY**
   - (A) comedy : tragedy
   - (B) tirade : criticism
   - (C) rhetoric : politics
   - (D) diatribe : speech
   - (E) paucity : emotion

4. **REPUTATION : SLANDER**
   - (A) predilection : favor
   - (B) inquisition : demand
   - (C) sanction : grant
   - (D) indictment : announce
   - (E) communication : garble

5. **SPIRIT : MAGNANIMOUS**
   - (A) criterion : first
   - (B) effort : prodigious
   - (C) edict : quixotic
   - (D) verbosity : redundant
   - (E) dearth : innocuous

MATCHING
Circle the one synonym or definition that best defines each word in bold type.

1. **defer**
   (A) pine tree
   (B) give way to
   (C) reduce in rank
   (D) abhor

2. **imply**
   (A) hint
   (B) infer
   (C) layer
   (D) insult

3. **thwart**
   (A) confuse
   (B) harm
   (C) foil
   (D) evade

4. **whet**
   (A) urge
   (B) illiterate pronoun
   (C) dampen
   (D) sharpen

5. **predilection**
   (A) natural preference
   (B) hasty decision
   (C) garbled speech
   (D) campaign jitters

6. **arduous**
   (A) complex
   (B) demanding
   (C) dubious
   (D) heartfelt

7. **apocryphal**
   (A) expeditious
   (B) fictitious
   (C) suspicious
   (D) Aloysius

8. **lethargy**
   (A) illness
   (B) slowness
   (C) paucity
   (D) langour

9. **explicit**
   (A) outside the law
   (B) overextended
   (C) beyond question
   (D) aboveboard

10. **redundant**
    (A) superfluous
    (B) exceedingly stupid
    (C) evanescent
    (D) backward

FIND THE ODDBALL
In each word group, cross out the oddball, the one unrelated word or phrase.

1. applaud   greet with cheers   acclaim   approve of   announce

2. strengthen   harden   moderate   temper   adjudicate

3. defer to   venerate   revere   admonish   respect

4. speech   brevity   conciseness   succinctness   pithiness

5. garrulous   loquacious   verbose   jargon   gabbiness

6. dirty   appalling   abominable   shockingly awful   heinous

7. worklike   everyday   commonplace   menial   mundane

8. transient   ephemeral   vanishing fast   vapor   evanescent

9. open to question   dubious   suspicious   doubtful   unreal

10. slightly wacko   idealistic   goal-oriented   quixotic

11. dearth   lack   supply   paucity   scarcity   scantiness

12. whiny   querulous   petulant   fretful   adorable

FILL IN THE BLANKS

From the choices offered below, select the word that best completes the meaning and logic of each sentence. Alter the word as needed to fit the sentence.

copious	saturate	prodigal	clamor	pervasive
deduce	waive	negligible	vilify	eclectic
prodigious	aesthetic	diatribe	conducive	vitriolic
capitulate	fluctuate	innocuous	tentative	

1. "The students who taught this unit are writing the quiz," said the history teacher. "I _____ all control over it."

2. The first question was tough, so I jotted a(n) _____ answer in the margin and decided to come back to it later.

3. Sitting by the window is _____ to thoughts of canoe trips and camping, but not to recalling facts for this test.

4. Getting ready for our yearly winter campout requires careful planning, shopping, and _____ amounts of food because the guys in our group are _____ eaters.

5. We don't let Arturo shop for groceries anymore because he was a _____ spender who bought everything in sight.

6. Although Arturo nearly bankrupted us, we really pigged out on the _____ assortment of groceries he'd purchased.

7. The wilderness of pines and piercingly blue skies in winter appeals to my _____ senses.

8. Last year the temperatures on our trip _____ from below zero at night to the high 30s in the daytime, and there was only a _____ amount of snow.

9. Although we adjusted to the _____ smell of mink that slowly permeated camp, we never _____ where it came from.

10. After a bear raided the food we thought we'd hoisted out of reach, James launched into a furious, _____ speech that _____ all bears. (I'll bet their ears are still burning.)

11. We ordered James to end the _____, and he eventually _____, subsiding into a fairly _____ mumbling as he accused the bears of lying in wait for us each year.

12. With the food mostly gone, our gear _____ with the gamy odor of mink, and our bodies _____ for burgers and hot showers, we packed up and went home to civilization.

Answers for this review lesson begin on page 205.

MORE VERBS TO LOVE

---

undermine • repudiate • enhance • hamper • expedite
• relegate • emulate • squander • rescind • solicit •
emanate • extricate

UNDERMINE v. *to weaken or destroy bit by bit; to sap the strength of by undercutting*
Nothing *undermines* your image like having a little brother tag along wherever you go. Eddie has been slowly *undermining* my patience too, ever since he learned to walk.

REPUDIATE v. *to disown, disclaim, reject, or refuse*
Of course, I always *repudiate* Eddie's determined efforts to follow me. He keeps tracking me like a shadow, however, despite my repeated, stubborn *repudiation*.

ENHANCE v. *to make better or more desirable in some way*
One day, I figured I'd *enhance* my chances of losing him if I ducked into a dark alley. Unfortunately, that idea only *enhanced* his interest in following me.

HAMPER v. *to get in the way of; to hinder or impede*
How could I *hamper* my dogged little pest? He was certainly *unhampered* by the evil eye I kept giving him.

EXPEDITE v. *to smooth or speed up a process; facilitate*
To *expedite* Eddie's departure, I offered him a dollar for ice cream. No way, I was told. As usual, some things just cannot be *expedited*, no matter what you try.

RELEGATE v. *to put away or aside; to shift to a less important place; to position by rank*
I thought about *relegating* my brother to a Pests' Dungeon, where he could never annoy me again, but I *relegated* that idea to the back of my mind as I watched his bike suddenly swerve toward the street.

JUG/JUNCT/JOIN = to join or to marry

subjugate—*to subdue or conquer (lit. "under the yoke")*
subjugated the wildest one
can't *subjugate* the weather

enjoin—*to command or order urgently; to forbid or prohibit*
enjoined by tradition from participating

Also: **conjugal, conjugate, junction, conjunction, juncture, join, adjoin, rejoinder, injunction**

EMULATE v. *to try to equal (or even exceed) an example; to imitate* n. **emulation**
He was trying to *emulate* me by popping wheelies as he'd seen me do in our driveway. I yelled, "Cut it out, twerp!" because my example was the wrong one to *emulate*.

SQUANDER v. *to use up or spend in an overgenerous or silly way; to dissipate or waste*
Startled by my yell, Eddie rammed his bike into a lamppost, and we *squandered* an hour trying to straighten his wheel. I had planned to *squander* the day in a much more enjoyable way than that, hanging out with my friends.

RESCIND v. *to cancel or annul; to repeal, call back*
"I wish I could *rescind* your right to be my brother," I grumbled, sweating over his crumpled bike. It was a mean remark, but I was too angry to *rescind* it at the time.

TORT/TORS = to twist, wring

tortuous—*winding or twisted, like a road; crooked, tricky*
a *tortuous* path up the hillside
a *tortuous* thought process

extort—*to get something from a person by using fear or force or unfair power; to obtain by intimidation*
extorted the information from him

Also: **retort, distort, torsion, torque, torture, torturous** *(cruel, like torture),* **tort** *(in law, a wrongful act)*

SOLICIT v. *to ask for time, money, or moral support; to lure into wrongdoing* adj. **solicitous**, *showing concern*

When I cooled down, I *solicitously* asked if he was okay after his scary adventure. The look I got in reply made me feel as dumb as the guy who tried to *solicit* donations of ice for Eskimos.

EMANATE v. *to seep forth (smells or ideas); to emit*

Fists balled at his sides, Eddie glared at me and *emanated* anger. My own fury dwindled as I saw how small and hurt he was. The noise of the streets engulfed us, and cars and buses *emanated* their foul odors as we confronted each other.

EXTRICATE v. *to free from an entanglement or awkward spot*

Eventually we got on our bikes, only to stop a few minutes later while Eddie *extricated* his shoelace from his bike gear. As I watched him, I finally accepted the fact that I'd never *extricate* myself from my little brother.

MEMORY FIX

Once more, write these words down and say each one aloud as you write its synonym or definition.

FILL IN THE BLANKS

From the list below, select the word that best completes the meaning and logic of each phrase. Alter the words as needed to be grammatically correct.

extricate	undermine	subjugate	extort
solicitous	relegate	emanate	rescind
emulate	expedite	enhance	enjoin

1. a bylaw that _____ anyone but club members from voting

2. found his authority _____ by their growing criticism

3. put in jail for _____ money from small shopkeep-ers

4. watching over the sick child with _____ eyes

5. heavenly smell that _____ each spring from honeysuckle

6. old order that was _____ and taken off the books

7. fly will never _____ himself from the spider's web

8. difficult, if not impossible, to _____ Jefferson's achievements

9. carefully printed address will _____ delivery

10. historical habit of the arrogant of _____ others less aggressive

11. _____ that old chair to the basement until it's fixed

12. ready sense of humor that _____ any personality

RHYME TIME

Choose the correct word from the list of words in this chapter for each blank in this truly corny poetry.

1. Our woeful human tendency to hate,
   I would like to and I do _____!

2. If I tell you not to _____,
   that means don't apply a damper
   to my one essential whim.
   For I won't be _____
   to the group whose lives are fated
   to be meaningless or grim.

3. I'll _____ my invitation to the dance,

    Unless you _____ the look of those pants!

4. Will and Orville were told not to _____

    Their time by aiming up yonder.

    But they wanted to fly,

    So they gave it a try.

    Of the outcome, we couldn't be fonder.

5. I'm obliged to report

    That your attempt to _____

    A confession from this dope

    Is a prospect without hope.

MATCHING

Match the words in column A with their synonyms or definitions in column B and write them down in the space provided.

	A	B
_____	1. expedite	tortuous
_____	2. dissipate	weaken gradually
_____	3. solicit	repeal
_____	4. hinder	forbid
_____	5. undermine	try to equal
_____	6. emanate	squander
_____	7. enjoin	ask for
_____	8. emulate	hamper
_____	9. twisted	facilitate
_____	10. rescind	seep out

Answers for this chapter begin on page 205.

LIST 17

AN ESTEEMED ASSORTMENT

---

esteem • disparity • catharsis • anomaly • censure •
antithesis • fallacy • indolence • fledgling • hindrance
• clemency • jeopardy

ESTEEM n. *high opinion of one's worth or character* v. **esteem,**
to value extremely
Because the British are known to *esteem* royalty, English diarist Samuel
Pepys (pronounced "peeps") jokingly wrote this about King Charles II:
"Methought it lessened my *esteem* of a king, that he should not be able
to command the rain."

DISPARITY n. *difference in type, quality, or quantity* adj.
disparate
Although we think there's a *disparity* between passion and reason, the
English poet John Donne blended them in his poetry. After all, the
perceived *disparity* between love and hate is believed to be two sides of
one coin.

CATHARSIS n. *a cleansing or purging that releases emotions*
adj. **cathartic**
A funeral is meant to be a *cathartic* event that allows us to vent our grief
openly and fully so that it is no longer a burden. Tears are one obvious
form of *catharsis*, of course.

ANOMALY n. *something different from the norm; irregularity
or paradox* adj. **anomalous**
As a night owl, I'm an *anomaly* in a family of early risers who turn into
pumpkins at 10 p.m. An irregularity of any kind usually sticks out, like
the *anomalous* black sheep.

CENSURE n. *stern or official condemnation* v. **censure**
"No man can justly *censure* or condemn another," wrote the
seventeenth-century English physician Sir Thomas Browne, "because
indeed no man truly knows another." Yes, but what would the media do
without *censure*?

GREG = crowd, flock, group

gregarious—*social and convivial; fond of groups*
  her bubbly, *gregarious* personality
  the *gregarious* elephant

egregious—*painfully noticeable; flagrant; outstandingly bad*
  egregious error
  disciplined the child's *egregious* behavior

Also: **congregate, congregation, aggregate, segregate**

ANTITHESIS n. *a direct opposite* adj. **antithetical**

The world has lots of "near opposites," but truly *antithetical* things are rare. War is the *antithesis* of peace, day the *antithesis* of night, and good the *antithesis* of evil.

FALLACY n. *incorrect idea; wrong assumption; an error* adj. **fallacious**

The idea behind the "pathetic *fallacy*" is that when you're under severe emotional strain, you're easy prey to *fallacious* impressions. For example, it's a *fallacy* to believe that nature rejoices along with you, just because you are happy.

INDOLENCE n. *supreme laziness or idleness; sloth*

Mom's last vacation was a study in *indolence*, as she put it. "I'm majoring in sloth this week, and I refuse to even move in that direction," she said, waving one *indolent* hand toward the kitchen.

NOV/NEO = new

novel—*new or original*
innovate—*to do something new*
  a *novel* idea
  novel solution
  a highly *innovative* plan

neophyte—*novice, beginner, tyro, newcomer, proselyte*
  a *neophyte* on the court
  fresh ideas from our *neophyte*

Also: **novelty, novice, novitiate, renovate, neon, neonatal, neologism**

FLEDGLING n. *a young bird with new flight feathers; an untested beginner; novice*
Every field has its *fledglings*—people who have the knowledge or equipment for a job but haven't yet proved themselves. Most *fledglings* are marked by an appealing enthusiasm.

HINDRANCE n. *an obstacle, impediment; something in the way* v. **hinder**, *to impede*
At leaf-raking time, Dude becomes a real *hindrance*. He darts wildly into our tidy leaf piles, scattering leaves everywhere and *hindering* the entire project of fall cleanup.

CLEMENCY n. *lenience or moderation in punishment; mercy* adj. **clement**, *mild (weather); merciful*
In *The Merchant of Venice*, Portia asks that justice be tempered with *clemency* for Antonio, who owes Shylock a pound of flesh. That famous soliloquy seeking a *clement* judgment begins, "The quality of mercy is not strain'd, It droppeth as the gentle rain from heaven. . . ."

JEOPARDY n. *an exposure to or possibility of danger*
Jeopardy began as the Latin phrase *jocus partitus*, tied game, then became French, *jeu parti*, meaning that the game's outcome was uncertain. Now when people are in *jeopardy* they are at risk or even in serious danger—except on the program of that name, which is still a game.

MEMORY FIX
Quick, take out a piece of paper and write down each of these new words along with a definition.

TRUE OR FALSE
Read each sentence to see how the words in this chapter are being used. Then mark **T** (true) or **F** (false) beside each.

1. Any business is managed best by a *neophyte*. _____

2. Acquiring knowledge helps to build *self-esteem*. _____

3. Repeated *censure* destroys self-esteem. _____

4. Rage is the *antithesis* of anger. _____

5. A stew is typically made from *disparate* ingredients. _____

6. There are noticeable *disparities* between identical twins.
   _____

7. The most prized assistant is an *indolent* one. _____

8. It's tough to hide an *anomaly* in the herd. Likewise, an *anomaly* in the herd had better have a tough hide. _____

9. When sad or depressed, spending time with comics Robin Williams and Billy Crystal might be very *cathartic*. _____

10. Thinking that I'll be a good diver because I'm a good swimmer is probably *fallacious* reasoning. _____

FIND THE ODDBALL

In each word group below, cross out the oddball, the one unrelated word or phrase.

1. regard   value   prize   outlook   esteem

2. honor   merciful   forgiving   lenient   indulgent

3. strong disapproval   urgency   condemnation   censure

4. symbiosis   antonymous pair   opposition   antithesis

5. master   tyro   neophyte   novice   fledgling proselyte

6. original   different   novel   fresh   hackneyed

7. sociable   convivial   aloof   social   gregarious

MATCHING

Find two synonyms or phrases in column B that explain each word in column A.

	A	**B**
_____	1. indolence	sociable
_____		obstacle
_____	2. clemency	paradox
_____		a purging
_____	3. catharsis	lenience
_____		error
_____	4.fallacy	neophyte
_____		idleness
_____	5. hindrance	a cleansing
_____		convivial
_____	6. anomaly	mercy
_____		flagrant
_____	7. fledgling	sloth
_____		irregularity
_____	8. gregarious	outstandingly bad
_____		novice
_____	9. novel	wrong assumption
_____		original
_____	10. egregious	impediment
_____		new

Answers for this chapter begin on page 206.

FEELING GOOD

---

benign • blithe • elation • appease • jocular •
effervescent • extol • placid • ameliorate • serene •
frivolous • assuage

BENIGN adj. *gentle, gracious, kind; benevolent in outlook; mild or favorable, not malignant*
The dermatologist smiled *benignly* and urged me to relax. "The results of the biopsies show that the moles we removed from your hand were *benign*, not malignant, Ted."

BLITHE adj. *cheerful, lighthearted; or, casual or heedless*
A while back, I strolled in around 2 a.m. from a party, whistling *blithely*, only to meet my parents in the kitchen. They were waiting up for me, and the look on their faces was anything but *blithe*.

ELATION n. *exultation; high spirits* v. **elate**
When I saw those furious faces, my *elation* quickly faded, and I felt myself turning red. I have turned red other times, when I was exercising hard or *elated* over something, but this was a different red altogether.

APPEASE v. *to quiet, calm, allay; to pacify or conciliate (refers to people or emotions, not conditions)*
I knew it was time to *appease* the folks, and in a hurry. I choose the truth because it was my only hope, as I saw it, of *appeasing* their anger.

JOCULAR adj. *jolly, fond of joking (L. joc = joke);* also, **jocose** *and* jocund = *merry, witty*
My folks are *jocular* people. Dad has even called home in the middle of the day to relate some *jocose* remark from a friend at work.

EFFERVESCENT adj. *bubbling with high spirits; exhilarated* v. **to effervesce** n. **effervescence**
Mom's usually an *effervescent* person, bubbling over with enthusiasm about one thing or another. It's hard to resist anybody whose spirit *effervesces* like that.

AM = to love; friend

amiable—*easy to get along with; friendly and good-natured*
a spaniel's gentle, *amiable* nature
an *amiable* settlement

amity—*friendship and good-will; harmony*
a nation known for *amity*
the natural *amity* of old friends

Also: **amicable, enamored, amorous, amatory, amateur, paramour**

EXTOL v. *to "sing" the praises of, glorify, praise highly*
I don't usually *extol* the virtues of my parents, but when I meet other kids' folks, I know I am luckier than most. Of course, my folks *extol* their terrific kids all the time, but you expect that of parents.

PLACID v. *calm in nature, not easily ruffled; quiet, serene*
I am quieter than my parents, not *placid* exactly, but not always joking around either. My friend Greg is so *placid* that people often wonder if he's asleep.

AMELIORATE v. *to improve or better (a condition)*
Anyway, to return to the night of the Big Bad Late Party, I was able to *ameliorate* the whole sticky situation by explaining to my folks that I'd met the perfect woman. Telling the truth doesn't always *ameliorate* a problem, but it's amazing how it has repeatedly helped me.

PATH/PAS = feeling, suffering, disease

apathy—*lack of feeling or interest; impassiveness; indifference*
an *apathetic* nod
unfortunate *apathy* toward the poor

dispassionate—*fair; not affected by strong feeling*
a *dispassionate* opinion
a carefully *dispassionate* review

Also: **sympathy, empathy, antipathy, pathos, pathetic, sociopath, passion, compassion, impassive, pathology**

SERENE adj. *extremely quiet, calm, and peaceful*
As I explained about meeting Beth, I saw Mom lean back against the kitchen wall and relax, gradually becoming more *serene*. She wasn't totally calm, not Mrs. *Serenity*-of-the-year or anything, but she was definitely calmer.

FRIVOLOUS adj. *not serious; inappropriately high-spirited; foolishly self-indulgent* n. **frivolity**
When I finished talking, Dad said, "Thanks, Ted. I wasn't in the mood for any *frivolous* excuses." I smiled, because at two in the morning he has never been in the mood for anything, let alone something *frivolous*!

ASSUAGE v. *to ease or relieve something that hurts or is worrisome; to quiet, pacify; to appease*
So that's my Parent-Management Tip of the Week, I guess: The best way to *assuage* your folks' worries is to tell them what really happened. *Assuaging* someone's fears isn't always this easy, of course, because sometimes truth is painful.

MEMORY FIX
Write each of these new words now, along with a synonym or definition for each. It helps to say them aloud as you write.

FIND THE SYNONYMS
From the word choices offered below, select the missing synonym for each numbered word group.

> amiable   benign   amity   apathetic   dispassionate
> jocular   elated   serene   frivolity   effervescent

1. joyous silliness   costly trifle   unseemly humor

_____

2. pleasant   easygoing   friendly   amicable _____

3. high-spirited   overjoyed   filled with pleasure

_____

4. emotionless   unaffected by feelings _____

5. revealing no emotion   impassive _____

6. bubbling with enthusiasm   exhilarated _____

7. placid   calm   quiet   peaceful   unflappable

_____

8. benevolent   kind   favorable   gentle _____

9. friendship   accord   harmonious relations _____

10. jocose   lighthearted   humorous   jocund _____

FILL IN THE BLANKS

Select the new word in this chapter that best completes the meaning and logic of each phrase. Remember to use the correct form of the word.

1. benefited from the _____ influence of the monks

2. a travelogue that _____ the many virtues of Spain

3. a nature so serene, so eternally _____, that I wondered if she had any passion at all

4. with more _____ than a bottle of soda pop

5. a serious attempt to _____ the deteriorating state of the building

6. a(n) _____ but enjoyable way to blow all of my allowance

7. amusing Noel Coward play, _____ Spirit, about a humorous, cheerful ghost

8. thoughtful talk that attempted to _____ our fears about the upcoming changes

9. announcing his promotion with obvious _____

10. a(n) _____ note meant to _____ Grandma after we'd made a mess in her yard

FIND THE ANTONYMS

Match up the opposites by writing them on the correct lines.

_____	1. elated	dispassionate
_____	2. impassive	censure
_____	3. appease	overwrought
_____	4. passionate	downcast
_____	5. extol	irritate
_____	6. sensible	effervescent
_____	7. placid	frivolous

Answers for this chapter begin on page 206.

MIGHTY OBVIOUS OPPOSITES

partial/impartial • potent/impotent • inflate/deflate • famous/infamous • savory/unsavory • tangible/ intangible • auspicious/inauspicious • discriminate/ indiscriminate • consent/dissent • neutral/biased

PARTIAL adj. *biased or even strongly disposed toward; or, referring to a portion of a whole*
IMPARTIAL adj. *unbiased, not prejudiced; fair, evenhanded*
At election time, journalists need to be *impartial* in their coverage of all candidates. Even if they're *partial* to one, they should avoid showing that *partiality* in print.

POTENT adj. *strong, powerful; effective (as "a potent remedy")*
IMPOTENT adj. *lacking effectiveness; weak, lacking strength*
Age proves to us that words are *potent* weapons. As kids we chanted, "Sticks and stones my break my bones, but words will never harm me." Yet we suspected way back then that words were far from *impotent*.

INFLATE v. *to blow or puff up, either literally or figuratively; to expand or enlarge, sometimes unwisely*
DEFLATE v. *to let the air out of, thereby reducing in size, either a tire or someone's ego*
As we *inflated* balloons to celebrate Greg's victory as class president, I could see his ego *inflating*, too. "Hey, buddy," I said, to *deflate* him a bit before he got too obnoxious, "there's a zit on your nose."

FAMOUS adj. *widely known; outstanding, noted, excellent* adv. **famously**, *very or extremely*
INFAMOUS adj. *of exceedingly bad repute; disgraceful* n. **infamy**
Our family has a set of widely diverse twins, one *famous* for his generosity, the other *infamous* for deceiving everyone he meets. That kind of *infamy* I can live without!

CRAC/CRAT = to rule

autocrat—*one who makes and executes the laws; dictator*
  iron rule of the *autocrat*
  a clearly *autocratic* decision

aristocracy—*a privileged class; certain well-qualified people; an upper class of hereditary nobility*
  the local *aristocracy*
  fine, *aristocratic* bearing

Also: **democrat, democracy, theocracy, plutocracy, aristocrat**

SAVORY adj. *very tasty, palatable; referring to a good reputation; edifying or mind-pleasing*
UNSAVORY adj. *smelling or tasting bad; morally repugnant or disgusting; distasteful*
In merrie olde England, a meat *savory* was a spiced meat dish served as an appetizer. Now, because the word's meaning has grown, you can be a person with a *savory* reputation (excellent) who enjoys *savory* foods (tasty) while writing a collection of *savory* essays (mind-pleasing). Of course, anything *unsavory* is highly suspect, like that fellow who has an *unsavory* reputation.

DEM = people

demagogue—*false leader who tells people what they want to hear, using popular prejudices to win approval*
  the latest *demagogue* in office
  empty talk of a *demagogue*

pandemic—*throughout an entire* (pan) *population* (dem)
  pandemic illness
  a tendency to become *pandemic*

Also: **epidemic, democrat, democracy, endemic, demographics**

TANGIBLE adj. *real, concrete, able to be touched (palpable); perceptible*
INTANGIBLE adj. *not concrete; impalpable yet real, such as cheerfulness*
Labeled a "decade of greed," the '80s were a time when people eagerly acquired impressive *tangible* property, such as luxury cars and huge houses. Perhaps the new century will see an emphasis on *intangible* assets, like concern for others.

AUSPICIOUS adj. *highly favorable; propitious* n. **auspice**, *a prophetic sign*
INAUSPICIOUS adj. *unfavorable; foreboding ill*
The Roman *auspex* divined the future by studying the flight and feeding patterns of birds. If the *auspices* were *auspicious*, he advised a ruler to act confidently. *Inauspicious* signs foretold trouble. When my car's engine overheated, I knew that was a very *inauspicious* sign.

DISCRIMINATE v. *to notice differences, distinguish clearly between objects or choices; to treat differently*
INDISCRIMINATE adj. *at random, without discrimination; haphazard*
I can easily *discriminate* among various pizzas and tell you which is best and why. I would never grab any old piece of pizza, making a totally *indiscriminate* choice, because pizza is important to me.

CONSENT n. *agreement; acceptance* v. **consent**, *to agree to*
DISSENT n. *disagreement* v. **dissent**, *to disagree*
Class presidents obtained the *consent* of each class before a large donated sum was spent on band uniforms and equipment. Of course, some sports fans *dissented*, but they were overruled for once.

NEUTRAL adj. *without bias or prejudice; neither for nor against*
BIASED adj. *prejudiced; having a distinct feeling one way or another*
Modern Sweden is a *neutral* country that has not taken sides in a war or funded a "war chest" like the United States. The U.S., *biased* in favor of democracy, has spent billions promoting that method of government and defending it.

MEMORY FIX

This time, write down only the words you DO NOT KNOW and their meanings. Say these words aloud as you write them.

WORDS IN CONTEXT

Write the meaning of each italicized word on the line provided.

1. the most *unsavory* concoction I ever saw

_____

2. an *inflated* idea of his own importance

_____

3. the immensity of the problem made her feel totally *impotent*

_____

4. always *partial* to something chocolate

_____

5. the *intangible* reward of their gratitude

_____

6. his A+ was an *auspicious* beginning for the year

_____

7. giving out candy with an *indiscriminate* hand

_____

8. Clay's ability to turn *dissent* into compromise

_____

9. choose consensus rather than the dictates of an *autocrat*

_____

10. a member of the feline *aristocracy*, unlike our Meatloaf

_____

TRUE OR FALSE

Read each sentence to see how the words in this chapter are being used. Then mark **T** (true) or **F** (false) beside each.

1. A *demagogue* needs both candor and sincerity. _____

2. One reason to select jurors with care is to eliminate *biased* individuals and choose *impartial* ones. _____

3. Vampires scoff at *potent* spells against them. _____

4. Fans hang around stage doors hoping for a glimpse of the most *infamous* stars. _____

5. I'd be eager to taste a *savory* dish offered as *tangible* proof of your culinary skills. _____

6. Mozart's talent was so great that it is sometimes difficult to *discriminate* between early works and later ones. _____

7. The various cold viruses are properly termed *pandemic*.

    _____

8. Blue skies are an *inauspicious* omen in the morning. _____

9. *Deflated* team spirits can translate into a quick loss of yardage on the football field. _____

10. The more you know about a subject, the harder it may be to remain totally *neutral*. _____

Answers for this chapter begin on page 206.

COMPLIMENT? NOT!

---

didactic • fickle • gullible • insipid • petty • incorrigible • officious • pompous • inane • willful • tedious • wanton

---

DIDACTIC adj. *instructive, designed to teach; morally "preachy"; pedantic*
The word *didactic* originated in Greece and meant "apt in teaching." Today, anything described as *didactic* is apt to be preachy, dull, or both.

FICKLE adj. *changeable, inconstant, irresolute; not steadfast*
The faithless behavior of a *fickle* lover is the subject of the old country-western favorite, "Your Cheatin' Heart." One sex is always accusing the other of being *fickle*.

GULLIBLE adj. *easily fooled; naive, ingenuous, innocent*
A *gullible* person swallows whatever you tell him, maybe down his gullet? And a *gull* is a fool or dupe who's easily decieved. Remember that *gullible* fellow who thought he was buying the Brooklyn Bridge for $24?

INSIPID adj. *lacking flavor, zip, or interest; dull, flat*
To French novelist Anatole France, "A tale without love is like beef without mustard: *insipid*." (What a thoroughly French analogy.) *Mais oui*, the world would be an infinitely more *insipid* place without love and mustard.

PETTY adj. *of minor importance; small-minded*
Near the end of *Macbeth*, King Macbeth says, "Tomorrow, and tomorrow, and tomorrow/Creeps in this *petty* pace from day to day," beginning a world-famous soliloquy. In modern use, anything *petty* is usually small-minded in nature.

INCORRIGIBLE adj. *extremely difficult to manage or control; delinquent, recalcitrant*
Having lived with two *incorrigible* pets, I understand this word. Our own *incorrigible* cat sleeps in the clothes dryer but doesn't enjoy tumbling about on high heat.

DOG/DOX = opinion, praise

dogmatic—*stubbornly opinionated; dictatorial; doctrinaire*
    the autocrat's *dogmatic* approach
    unpopular *dogmatic* style

orthodox—*according to traditional teaching or established religious doctrine; "by the book"*
    in an *orthodox* manner
    comfortable, *orthodox* presentation

Also: **dogma, doxology, paradox, heterodox**

OFFICIOUS adj. *self-important and meddlesome; interfering; impertinent*
An *officious* person is a "buttinski"; you know the type. As writer Ivan Krylov put it, "Heaven save you from a foolish friend; the too *officious* fool is worse than any foe."

POMPOUS adj. *puffed up with self-importance; arrogant*
Just as unpopular as the "officious fool" is the "*pompous* ass"— someone dying to impress you with his importance or knowledge. Unfortunately, one afflicted with *pomposity* is all too often known for verbosity as well.

INANE adj. *witless, empty, insipid, "dopey"*
The best *inane* giggle in show business belonged to Butterfly McQueen, who played the part of a witless young girl in *Gone With the Wind*. Only a fine actress like Ms. McQueen could have created such a believably *inane* yet lovable character.

DOC/DACT = to teach

docile—*easily controlled or taught; compliant, tractable, amenable, obedient*
    a *docile* breed of cows
    a sweet, *docile* child

indoctrinate—*to teach the basics; teach a specific point of view*
    indoctrinated by church leaders
    indoctrinate new members

Also: **doctor, doctrine, doctrinaire, didactic**

WILLFUL adj. *headstrong; stubbornly self-willed; unruly*
Incorrigible pets like ours are *willful* ones, determined to do what they want just like young children. Once when Eddie didn't get his way, he ground a banana into our new rug, a *willful* act that got him into a lot of trouble.

TEDIOUS adj. *tiresome, boring; seeming too long or dull*
Anatole France, a most quotable satirist, wrote that "historical books which contain no lies are extremely *tedious*." History is fascinating if you like it, of course, and only *tedious* if you don't.

WANTON adj. *arousing sexual desire; lacking human kindness (as in "wanton cruelty"); malicious; unchecked (as in "a wanton growth of weeds")*
Behind all the meanings of *wanton* is the idea of uncontrolled behavior. Not all things need control, of course, such as wildflowers that grow on the hillsides in *wanton* profusion.

MEMORY FIX
As with the last list, write down only the words you don't know or are unsure about. As you note their meanings, say each word aloud.

SUBSTITUTION
Replace each italicized word or phrase with the correct new word from this chapter.

1. The salesman delivered a *teaching* talk that was surprisingly interesting and convincing. _____

2. "I guess I'm sort of *easily deceived*," my cousin Sara confessed later, hiding her latest purchase behind her back.

   _____

3. "Maybe I'm even *impossible to control*," she went on miserably, "because I always fall for a good spiel." _____

4. I shrugged and gave her an *empty, silly* smile, but her *loose and uncontrolled* purchases were getting on my nerves.

   _____ _____

5. "Well," I harrumphed, "I don't mean to be *tiresome or boring*, but shouldn't you quit this?" _____

6. Sara gave me a smile that was anything but *obedient* and said, "You don't need to act so *self-important!*"

   _____   _____

7. I mumbled, "Sorry. I hate people who are *meddlesome and interfering.*" _____

8. "That's better," she replied. "It's not like you to be *small-minded*, either, so let's forget it." _____

9. "Sure. Just put that food grinder away with all the others," I said, not caring that I sounded *dictatorial.* _____

10. Defeated, she gave me a(n) *zestless* smile. "Ah, clever cousin. How did you know it was another food grinder?"

    _____

MATCHING

From the list below, find two synonyms for each numbered word and write them in on the correct lines.

pedantic	unchecked	naive	established	delinquent
inconstant	flavorless	preachy	tractable	ingenuous
witless	recalcitrant	insipid	traditional	inhumane
compliant	changeable	dull	interfering	impertinent

1. fickle _____   _____

2. gullible _____   _____

3. insipid _____   _____

4. didactic _____   _____

5. incorrigible _____   _____

6. inane _____   _____

7. wanton _____   _____

8. orthodox _____   _____

9. docile _____   _____

10. officious _____   _____

FIND THE ODDBALL

In each word group, cross out the oddball, the one unrelated word or phrase.

1. mean-spirited   ugly   unimportant   minor   petty

2. unsavory   self-important   arrogant   pompous   puffed-up

3. unruly   willful   stubbornly determined   headstrong   biased

4. theoretical   traditional   orthodox   established

5. instruct   train   indoctrinate   teach a doctrine   moderate

6. fickle   doctrinaire   dogmatic   opinionated   dictatorial

Answers for this chapter begin on page 207.

LISTS 16-20 REVIEW

Just in case a few words from lists 16 through 20 have gone astray, it's time to review. Read those lists again, then you can whip through these few reminder-type exercises.

ANALOGIES

Circle the one word pair in each list below that expresses the same relationship as the pair in capital letters.

1. **REASONING : FALLACIOUS**
   - (A) logic : dispassionate
   - (B) behavior : docile
   - (C) ruling : orthodox
   - (D) judgment : biased
   - (E) demeanor : amiable

2. **INFAMY : CENSURE**
   - (A) studies : indoctrinate
   - (B) pettiness : extricate
   - (C) virtue : extol
   - (D) amity : savor
   - (E) novelty : enjoin

3. **PLEASANT : JOCULAR**
   - (A) insipid : inane
   - (B) famous : cultured
   - (C) serene : placid
   - (D) clement : mild
   - (E) contented : blithe

4. **DEMAGOGUE : SINCERITY**
   - (A) neophyte : experience
   - (B) feline : indolence
   - (C) aristocracy : dogma
   - (D) conflict : jeopardy
   - (E) autocrat : pomposity

5. **EFFERVESCENT : ELATION**
   - (A) overjoyed : emulation
   - (B) deflated : repudiation
   - (C) incorrigible : apathy
   - (D) indecision : clemency
   - (E) impassive : discrimination

6. **CONFIDENCE : UNDERMINE**
   - (A) capital : squander
   - (B) fears : assuage
   - (C) donation : solicit
   - (D) consent : extort
   - (E) embankment : erode

MATCHING ANTONYMS

Match the antonyms by writing the correct opposite beside each numbered word.

_____	1. intangible	ominous, foreboding
_____	2. officious	similarity
_____	3. wanton	ineffective
_____	4. expedite	agreement
_____	5. ameliorate	engrossing, absorbing
_____	6. auspicious	disgrace
_____	7. dissent	implicate
_____	8. tedious	concrete
_____	9. potent	aggravate
_____	10. esteem	humble
_____	11. disparity	carefully controlled
_____	12. extricate	hinder

FIND THOSE SYNONYMS

On the lines provided, write the two best synonyms from this list of words to complete each numbered word group.

repeal	enjoin	unfeeling	impede	assuage
vacillating	hinder	inconstant	amicable	insipid
conciliate	novice	call back	crooked	empty
command	tortuous	gregarious	beginner	apathetic

1. hamper _____ obstruct _____

2. rescind _____ annul _____

3. _____ forbid _____ prohibit

4. _____ twisted _____ winding

5. fledgling _____ tyro _____

6. sociable _____ convivial _____

7. _____ fickle _____ changeable

8. _____ appease _____ pacify

9. impassive _____ indifferent

_____

10. inane _____ silly _____

GOOD WORDS GET AROUND

From the words listed below, fill in the blanks in these quotations.

alleviates   squander   petty   placid
frivolous   dogmatic   undermining impartial

1. "To waste, to destroy our natural resources, to skin and exhaust the land instead of using it so as to increase its usefulness, will result in _____ in the days of our children the very prosperity which we ought by right to hand down to them amplified and developed."
—Theodore Roosevelt, address to Congress, 1907

2. "Pale Death with _____ tread beats at the poor man's cottage door and at the palace of kings."
—Horace, Roman poet and satirist

3. "Dost thou love life? Then do not _____ time; for that's the stuff life is made of."
—Benjamin Franklin, *Poor Richard's Almanack*

4. "There is a strange charm in the thoughts of a good legacy . . . which wondrously _____ the sorrow that men would otherwise feel for the death of friends."
—Miguel Cervantes, *Don Quixote*

5. "I think I could turn and live with animals, they are so
   _____ and self-contained."
   —Walt Whitman, *Song of Myself*

6. "One who is serious all day will never have a good time, while
   one who is _____ all day will never establish a
   household."
   —Ancient Egyptian maxim

7. "When people are least sure, they are often most
   _____." (Look for irony here.)
   —John Kenneth Galbraith, American economist

8. "Why, man, he [Caesar] doth bestride the narrow world
   Like a Colossus; and we _____ men
   Walk under his huge legs, and peep about
   To find ourselves dishonourable graves."
   —Shakespeare, *Julius Caesar*

Answers for this review lesson begin on page 207.

AH, THE PRUDENT PURITANS

---

frugal • exemplary • diligent • prudent • scrupulous • parochial • pious • discreet • thrifty • solemn • pragmatic • steadfast

---

FRUGAL adj. *careful in using resources; sparing, thrifty*
Since I got my car, which eats cash, I've had to be *frugal* in all my spending. I can't keep this money-guzzler going unless *frugality* is my motto from now on.

EXEMPLARY adj. *serving as a model; commendable*
I had an *exemplary* month recently—didn't buy any extras—but did the car reward me with *exemplary* behavior? Hardly. It blew its head gasket.

DILIGENT adj. *showing painstaking care and attention*
I'll have to slave *diligently* for months to pay off this repair, and I bet it was my fault. The engine overheated because I wasn't *diligent* about keeping the radiator full.

PRUDENT adj. *shrewd and careful in managing things; wise; discreet, circumspect; also, frugal*
Luckily I know a *prudent* auto mechanic, Raoul, who owns a small local garage. Raoul hires only the best repairmen and *prudently* stocks rebuilt parts as well.

SCRUPULOUS adj. *showing painstaking care; extremely attentive to detail or to morality*
"A real mechanic," says Raoul, "pays *scrupulous* attention to details. I examine every connection, every hose, *scrupulously*, because overlooking even one thing can be disastrous."

PAROCHIAL adj. *of narrow, limited scope; provincial; referring to a church parish*
In addition to his ownership of the garage, Raoul has a *parochial* job as a lay priest. Until I got to know him, I had a totally uninformed and *parochial* view of his religion.

GEN = kind, race, birth, cause

congenial—*having kindred tastes; like-minded; sociable*
   a pleasant, *congenial* fellow
   having a *congenial* outlook

generic—*universal, general; referring to a group or class*
   a bottle of *generic* aspirin
   a *generic* form of gelatin

Also: **ingenuous *(naive)*, engender *(foster, begin)*, gentleman, disingenuous *(faking honesty)*, homogeneous** (The **gen** words love to appear on SATs.)

PIOUS adj. *noticeably religious, sometimes to the point of hypocrisy; or, honestly religious and devoted* n. **piety**
Even if he is a lay priest, Raoul doesn't go around making *pious* comments about religion all the time. His *piety* is real, not phony; anyone can tell how sincere he is.

DISCREET adj. *showing good sense (prudence) in behavior; circumspect; modest (as in "discreet of speech")* n. **discretion**
Dad and I had one of those *discreet*, father-son talks last night, away from the rest of the family. Of course, any kid should use some *discretion* when he's talking to a parent, but Dad and I have always been pretty open with each other.

CRED = to believe

credible—*believable, trustworthy; worthy of being believed*
   a *credible* witness
   would never question his *credibility*

credulous—*willing to believe almost anything; gullible*
   a young, *credulous* person
   a *credulous* dog, easily fooled

Also: **incredible *(amazing)*, incredulous *(unbelieving)*, credit, creditable, discredit, credentials**

THRIFTY adj. *extremely careful with money; provident, sparing, frugal* n. **thrift**
"You'll have to be extra *thrifty*," Dad said, "to pay off a repair bill that size. I've always been a rather *thrifty* fellow myself, so I can afford to lend you money at no interest—how's that?"

SOLEMN adj. *extremely serious; sober, sedate*
I'd already worked out a payment schedule with Raoul, so I made Dad a *solemn* promise that he didn't have to worry about me and my car. "I admire the way you're handling this, Ted," Dad said, pretty *solemn* himself.

PRAGMATIC adj. *practical, not idealistic; sensible* n. **pragmatist (person) and pragmatism**
I thought I'd made a normal, *pragmatic* arrangement to pay my bill, so I was surprised by Dad's praise. Now that I own a car that eats money, I'm forced to operate in a more *pragmatic*, thoughtful way.

STEADFAST adj. *not apt to change; steady, faithful, loyal*
My friend Greg really fits the word *steadfast*, even if it sounds old-fashioned. In fact, he's such a *steadfast* friend that he's paying part of my repair bill, because he always depends on me for his transportation.

MEMORY FIX
On a separate piece of paper, just like before, write down each word in this list along with a definition and say each one aloud.

FILL IN THE BLANKS
Select the new word from this chapter that best completes the meaning and logic of each sentence. Alter the form of the word as needed for sense.

1. She's so _____ she'd believe anything you tell her.

2. Jana needs to give _____ attention to that experiment so that each chemical is added at the right time.

3. _____ is a perfect antonym of fickle.

4. The prodigal spender is the antithesis of the
   _____ soul who lives a life based on
   _____.

5. A crazy idealist like Don Quixote is clearly not a
   _____.

6. Little Lord Fauntleroy and Miss Goody Two-Shoes were known for
   their _____ conduct.

7. Turn six words from this lesson into nouns, and you have six
   virtues esteemed by the Puritans: _____,
   _____, _____,
   _____, _____, and
   _____.

8. The Puritanical outlook was unfortunately _____,
   an irony when you consider that they settled the colonies to
   escape prejudice.

9. The Puritans are always portrayed as a somber lot, known for
   their _____ of manner and
   _____ clothing to match.

10. It took only a brief time to establish the _____ of
    _____ drugs, which are the same as the name
    brands but without the big price tag.

ADD THE SYNONYMS

From this chapter's word list, definitions, and synonyms, complete each
numbered word group.

1. thrifty _____ prudent _____

2. circumspect _____ discreet

3. of a church parish _____ provincial

4. praiseworthy commendable _____ acting as a model

5. attentive to detail _____ showing painstaking care

6. loyal _____ steady _____

7. like-minded _____ sociable _____

TRUE OR FALSE
Read the sentences below and then mark **T** (true) or **F** (false) for each.

1. The most effective liar is a wholly *credible* one. _____

2. You might as well dismiss an accountant who's been accused of *scrupulousness*. _____

3. The name THRIFT DRUG encourages you to think it will be a *prudent* place to shop. _____

4. Puritans would have preferred a little levity or frivolity in church compared to all that *solemnity* they endured. _____

5. Say that a president is a *pragmatist* and he's doomed. _____

6. The older you get, the more *credulous* you're apt to be. _____

7. Because *generic* products don't pay for advertising, they can be sold at lower costs. _____

8. The best college roommate would be a *congenial* person. _____

Answers for this chapter begin on page 208.

OUT OF THIS WORLD

---

clairvoyant • chimera • eccentric • karma • enigma • vicarious • hypothetical • cryptic • esoteric • oblivious • utopia • elusive

---

CLAIRVOYANT n. *one who perceives far more than the normal five senses would explain; a seer* adj. **extraordinarily perceptive** n. **clairvoyance**
In the days before science took hold, people turned to a *clairvoyant* for explanations of the inexplicable. In the twentieth century, only those who study paranormal psychology are comfortable with the possibility of true *clairvoyance* in humans.

CHIMERA (ki-'mir-e) n. *a Greek mythic being with a lion's head, goat's body, and a serpent's tail* adj. **chimerical,** *fanciful, imaginary, improbable, foolish*
"What a *chimera* then is man! What a novelty! . . . the glory and the shame of the universe," said Blaise Pascal, a seventeenth-century French mathematician and philosopher. For centuries, philosophers have debated the *chimerical* nature of humankind.

ECCENTRIC adj. *decidedly odd or unusual; aberrational* n. *an odd person* pl. **eccentricities,** *oddities, aberrations*
Always try for the part of an *eccentric* in a play, because a quirky character is easier to portray and usually steals the show. Remember the hilarious *eccentricities* of Oscar and Felix in *The Odd Couple*?

KARMA n. *your life force that determines your fate or destiny in the next life (Hinduism, Buddhism)*
What is *karma* for the Buddhist is *kismet* for the Arab or Turk. "You must mean predestination," says the Presbyterian. Whether we call it *karma* or something else, everyone would like to explain why life unfolds as it does.

CED/CESS/CEDE = to go, yield

precedent—*any model for that which follows; antecedent*
a legal *precedent*
following a well-known *precedent*

intercede—*to come between disputing parties; mediate*
wish someone would *intercede* and end this conflict

Also: **cede, exceed, excess, accede, recede, concede, secede, secession, succeed, process, recess, ancestor, antecedent**

ENIGMA n. *a riddle hard to puzzle out; conundrum; mystery*
Early in World War II, Churchill broadcast to his English audience: "I cannot forecast to you the action of Russia. It is a riddle wrapped in a mystery inside an *enigma*." And for the modern generation, Russia still appears *enigmatic*.

VICARIOUS adj. *felt or experienced secondhand, through someone else or through another medium*
Riding a roller coaster is a real thrill, not a *vicarious* experience. Anyone wanting *vicarious* terror can go to the movies or turn on the TV.

HYPOTHETICAL adj. *based on a hypothesis (a logical theory) rather than on reality; conjectural*
Most of our accepted scientific laws began as a logical conjecture, a *hypothetical* "What if . . ." that led to experiments that proved the initial *hypothesis*.

CRYPTIC adj. *obscure; intentionally mysterious*
My buddies from Y camp recalled a *cryptic* code we invented one summer. Every summer after that we sent each other *cryptic* messages, especially when we were planning a trip across the lake to the girls' camp.

CHRON = time

anachronism—*a thing out of place in time*
an *anachronism* like the steam engine or a peddler's cart

chronic—*habitual, repetitive, long-lasting, frequent*
a *chronic* worrywart
seems to have a *chronic* cold

Also: **chronology, synchronize, chronological, chronicle**

ESOTERIC adj. *of knowledge belonging to initiated people*
Twins often develop an *esoteric* language that no one else understands. When I listen to Dad and some of his chemist friends talking, I think that advanced chemistry has its own *esoteric* vocabulary, too.

OBLIVIOUS n. *totally unaware (usu. with "of" or "to")*
Mom accuses us kids of being *oblivious* to dirt and mess. It's not that we're *oblivious* exactly, it's just that we're more skilled at ignoring that stuff than most adults.

UTOPIA n. *a place where everything about life is perfect*
Meaning "nowhere" in Greek, *utopia* is a place so perfect that it's a pity it exists only in an old novel. (Dystopia was the place where everything was as bad as possible.) A great deal of literature centers on *utopian* longings for an ideal world.

ELUSIVE adj. *apt to evade pursuit or definition (as "an elusive thought"); hard to pin down, identify* v. **elude**
"We seek him here, we seek him there,
Those Frenchies seek him everywhere.
Is he in heaven?—Is he in hell?
That demmed, *elusive* Pimpernel?"
Throughout this swashbuckeling novel by Orczy, the Scarlet Pimpernel made it his business to *elude* his captors.

MEMORY FIX

As before, write down each word you don't know, with definitions for each, and say them all aloud.

SUBSTITUTION

Replace each italicized word or phrase with the correct word from this chapter's word and root lists. Change the word's form if necessary for grammatical correctness.

1. dispute could last forever unless you *come in between*

   _____

2. a wounded man, *unaware of* the fight continuing around him

   _____

3. gave me a *mysterious* glance I couldn't interpret

_____

4. not an actual project yet, purely *based on conjecture*

_____

5. a *fantastic* plan that had no prayer of being successful

_____

6. lost language of the Druids, along with all their *known only to certain people* lore _____

7. don't know whether it was dumb luck or simply my *destiny*

_____

8. the *hard to track* fragrance of an elegant perfume

_____

9. *extremely odd* behavior that is without *an antecedent*

_____   _____

10. a(n) *frequent* yearning for *a perfect place*

_____   _____

TRUE OR FALSE

Read each sentence to see how the words in this chapter are being used. Then mark **T** (true) or **F** (false) beside each one.

1. Shakespeare's reference to a clock on the wall in *Julius Caesar* is an example of an *anachronism* in literature. _____

2. Cassandra the *Clairvoyant* would be a good name for the Trojan woman who said, ''Beware of Greeks bearing gifts.'' _____

3. The influence of gravity remains a *hypothetical* topic, still under discussion at Dr. Newton's house. _____

4. It hardly requires any *esoteric* information to interpret the Dead Sea scrolls. _____

5. If you're reading a book and fall downstairs, blame it on your bad *karma*, not just inattention. _____

6. Nothing is easier to unravel than a classic *enigma*. _____

7. If I allude to your successful stickup at the bank around my police sergeant uncle, you'd better get ready to *elude* his pursuit.
_____

MATCHING
Circle the two words or phrases that best explain the meaning of each word in bold type.

1. **unprecedented**   illegal   without example   annoying   novel

2. **clairvoyant**   weird   perceptive   a seer   persnickety

3. **eccentric**   unacceptable   fruity   aberrational   odd

4. **cryptic**   undecipherable   enigmatic   deadly   referring to burial

5. **oblivious**   "out to lunch"   clueless   confused   panicky

6. **intercede**   debate   intervene   dispute   mediate

7. **chronic**   repetitive   infectious   long-lasting   tardy

8. **vicarious**   exciting   lively   secondhand   substitutionary

9. **utopian**   ideal   unreal   perfect   impossible

10. **chimerical**   frightening   fanciful   miraculous   imaginary

Answers for this chapter begin on page 208.

LIST 23

BIG, FAT, GLORIOUS ADJECTIVES

virulent • whimsical • voluminous • ubiquitous • turbulent • haphazard • precocious • vindictive • unimpeachable • voracious • homogeneous • incongruous

VIRULENT adj. *full of malignant or evil intent; noted for fast, powerful, often fatal progress*
Tuberculosis, always a *virulent* disease, keeps coming back for another round. Though streptomycin cured the old strains, new and more *virulent* ones require new medication.

WHIMSICAL adj. *based on a whim or fancy; capricious*
Sometimes a *whimsical* longing for the ocean comes over me, and a bunch of us pile in the car and head out, even in winter. The occasional *whimsical* idea makes life more fun.

VOLUMINOUS adj. *extremely large in volume or size; also, numerous (as in "voluminous notes")*
You don't see *voluminous* skirts anymore, except on some wedding dresses. The only *voluminous* thing in my life right now is the pile of notes for my history paper on the Supreme Court.

UBIQUITOUS adj. *seemingly everywhere; widespread*
MacDonald's restaurants, *ubiquitous* today, were scarce just twenty-five years ago. Now the chain has flung its *ubiquitous* Golden Arches over all of Europe, even Russia.

TURBULENT adj. *marked by roiling and turmoil and unrest; seething, agitated*
The last half of our senior year is a *turbulent* time when so much is going on. This *turbulence* fills our minds, too, so that finding ways to relax is critical.

ANIMA = mind, soul, spirit

animosity—*hatred, antagonism, ill will, enmity*
    an *animosity* that went back in time
    unjustified *animosity*

equanimity—*coolness or evenness of disposition; balance*
    admired the *equanimity* that never deserted him

Also: **animal, animus, animated, unanimous, magnanimous,
pusillanimous** *(cowardly)*

HAPHAZARD adj. *unplanned; happening by chance, at random;
aimless* (hap = *luck or chance*)
The "hap" words are strewn *haphazardly* throughout the English
language. Consider, for example, *happen, happenstance, mayhap,
mishap, happy-go-lucky,* and *perhaps.* Originally, *happy* meant "lucky."
It's not just a *haphazard* connection, either; of course you'd be happy if
you were lucky.

PRECOCIOUS adj. *showing very early mental development (L. =
"precooked" or "prematurely ripe")*
Everyone hates baby-sitting a kid whose parent brags, "Oh, he's always
been *precocious.*" The early mastery of language and logic by the
precocious child is a lousy excuse for rude behavior.

VI/VIT/VIV = life

viable—*capable of living; able to work or develop acceptably
or even well*
    a *viable* fetus
    a *viable* product
    a *viable* candidate

convivial—*friendly and lively of spirit, party-loving*
    a noisy, *convivial* gathering
    her open, *convivial* nature

Also: **vital, vitamin, revitalize, vitality, vivid, revive,
vivisection, vivacity, vivacious**

VINDICTIVE adj. *eager for revenge; spiteful*
A *vindictive* spirit keeps a fight going, such as the famous Hatfield-McCoy feud in Appalachia. And isn't there something awfully *vindictive* about the ancient code of Hammurabi, which read, "An eye for an eye; a tooth for a tooth"?

UNIMPEACHABLE adj. *blameless, irreproachable; not open to accusation*
For my history paper, I went to an *unimpeachable* source of Supreme Court information: a sitting Justice. If a Justice's honor isn't absolutely *unimpeachable*, then no one's is.

VORACIOUS adj. *insatiably hungry for something; ravenous*
Kids who "tear up" the SATs and PSATs are the ones who've always been *voracious* readers. Greg's been a *voracious* eater for the last six years; now he's working on the reading.

HOMOGENEOUS adj. *being the same or alike throughout (lit. "the same kind"); also,* homogenous
Countries such as Sweden and Denmark tend to be extremely *homogeneous*, while the United States is less *homogenized* every day as the unhappy from afar find refuge here. Diversity of people makes life more interesting, but it is also more challenging than *homogeneity*.

INCONGRUOUS adj. *seeming out of place or unsuited*
A tuxedo would look totally *incongruous* in our school, except on Live Character Day. That day, we all dressed as our favorite literary character, and nothing seemed *incongruous*, especially not the terrific pig costume I wore as Wilbur.

MEMORY FIX
You know the routine. Write down each word you don't know, along with its definition, and say each word aloud.

FILL-IN CHART

Fill in the missing boxes with information learned in this chapter.

Word	Prefix/Root	Two Synonyms/ Definition
1.	**dic/dict** = say	revengeful,
2. turbulent	**turb** = agitate	
3.	**homo** = same **gen** = kind	same or alike throughout
4.	**anim** = spirit, soul	enmity,
5.	**hap** = luck, chance	
6.	**equ** = equal, same **anim** = spirit, soul	
7. virulent	**virus** = poison	
8. convivial	**con** = with; **viv** = life	
9.	**ubique** = everywhere	everywhere,
10. precocious	**pre** = before **coquere** = cooked	

RHYME TIME

Complete these lines of admittedly awful poetry with words from this chapter's list.

1. In the narrow coal shaft, hunting bituminous
   Forswear all garments considered _____.

2. Vicki suffered for hours from insects _____,
   She dug at the bites and swore, Goodness Gracious!
   Smearing her body with calamine lotion
   Was more than just a _____ notion.

3. It's an overused buzzword; I refuse to be liable,
    That tired, _____ adjective

    _____.

4. Our purebred came with papers _____,
    Sad to say, he has proved unteachable.

5. Students teaching classes is not an _____
    thought,
    We remember well what our peers have taught.

WORD ANALYSIS

Fill in the most logical word for each sentence, choosing from among the words presented in this chapter.

1. The child who is reading at age three is usually described as

    _____.

2. In the middle of a memorial service, giddy laughter would seem
    not only _____, but also irreverent.

3. Thomas á Becket, who did not accede to all of Henry II's wishes,
    was murdered in Canterbury Cathedral not long after Henry
    allegedly cried, "Who will rid me of the t_____
    priest?"

4. Elementary kids have a _____ appetite for
    information about dinosaurs.

5. You can tell that comedian Robin Williams gives in to
    _____ flights of fancy as they occur to him, ad
    libbing with a brilliance given only to a few.

6. Universally, people revere magnanimity and fear those with a
    _____ streak.

Answers for this chapter begin on page 209.

GOULASH

---

paradigm • unscathed • iconoclast • kindle • elaborate • tacit • peripheral • deter • propensity • discord • precipitate • unethical

---

PARADIGM n. *something serving as a model or ideal*
For years, our class unknowingly acted as a *paradigm* for classes after us. We didn't plan to be a model class, but we gradually realized that we were the acknowledged *paradigm*.

UNSCATHED adj. *unharmed, uninjured, untouched* adj. **scathing**, *bitterly severe, caustic*
No class is perfect, and ours won't graduate *unscathed*. This spring, our most outspoken students delivered some *scathing* criticism of the school to local newspaper reporters.

ICONOCLAST n. *one who criticizes established ideas or traditions (Gr. = image destroyer)*
These talkative students were known *iconoclasts*, of course, who'd rebelled for various reasons all through school. But we understood their *iconoclastic* views from long association and had always respected their ideas.

KINDLE v. *to start burning; to spark interest or curiosity*
Nothing *kindles* the interest of the public like a hot newspaper story. Our classmates' best suggestions for school reform *kindled* a desire in several parents to begin discussions with the school administration.

ELABORATE v. *to spell out specifically, in detail* adj. *detailed or complex; carefully planned*
Those interested parents asked our reform-minded classmates to *elaborate* on their ideas. While some of their concepts were too *elaborate* to implement, many of their suggestions met with approval, even requests for further *elaboration*.

SED/SESS/SID = to sit or be still

assiduous—*marked by careful, diligent attention; persistent*
  assiduously cleaning his fur
  giving it *assiduous* attention

insidious—*dangerous but appealing; slow but steady in effect; subtle; settling in unnoticed (as in "an insidious disease")*
  an *insidious* illness
  the *insidious* lure of gambling

Also: **sedentary, sediment, supersede, preside, subsidy, dissident, resident, session, obsession, sedate**

TACIT adj. *understood though not spoken; silent*
Students and parents arrived at a *tacit* agreement that the parents would advance these novel ideas. Everyone *tacitly* acknowledged that parents would receive more serious attention from school officials.

PERIPHERAL adj. *around the edge or periphery; auxiliary; of minor, not central, importance*
The parents' committee decided to deal with only a few central issues and to ignore the *peripheral* ones. Just as *peripheral* (side) vision is less critical than forward vision, some of the students' ideas were less important.

DETER v. *to hinder or prevent from acting; to inhibit, turn aside or discourage* n. **deterrent**
Nothing would *deter* my parents from joining this group of adults bent on change. I had hoped that my begging for noninvolvement would be a *deterrent*, but it wasn't.

TEND/TENS/TENT = to stretch

tenuous—*slight and insubstantial; flimsy, weak*
  only a *tenuous* grasp of the subject
  new and *tenuous* idea

extenuating—*mitigating; reducing in severity or importance*
  an *extenuating* circumstance that explained her lateness

Also: **tendency, extend, extension, portent, portentous, contend, contentious, tension, tense, pretense**

PROPENSITY n. *strong natural leaning or preference*
Have you noticed how your parents have a *propensity* for getting involved when you wish they wouldn't? The natural *propensity* of ostriches is to stick their heads in the sand, hoping to go unnoticed, but parents sure aren't like that.

DISCORD n. *lack of agreement or harmony; strife, tension*
The night the parents met with the school officials was marked at first by *discord*. The seeds of this *discord* had been sown by the newspaper story, of course.

PRECIPITATE v. *to cause to begin in an abrupt manner* adj. *unwisely fast, impetuous, headlong*
Although the newspaper article *precipitated* the parents' involvement with school policy, no one at the meeting wanted to plunge *precipitately* into massive changes.

UNETHICAL adj. *lacking moral principles (ethics)*
Closed meetings of public boards are *unethical* in our state. The "Sunshine Laws" insist that the operations—and therefore the *ethics*—of ruling boards should be open to scrutiny by their employers, the taxpayers.

MEMORY FIX
Now's the time to write down each word in this chapter that you don't know, along with its definition. Say each word aloud too. Remember why you're doing this? WRITING FIXES WORDS IN MIND.

FILL IN THE BLANKS
From the new words in this chapter, select the one that best completes the meaning and logic of each phrase. Be sure to use the right form of each word.

1. there'll be a reason, some _____ explanation

2. always questioned authority, a(n) _____ from birth

3. suspected of _____ behavior in office

4. hoping to _____ a creative fire to last all autumn

5. a real enigma that needs precise _____ (use the noun)

6. didn't actually say yes, but nodded in _____ approval

7. a(n) _____ weed that seemed to spread overnight

8. so weak now that she has but a(n) _____ hold on life

9. cannot do drugs and expect to escape _____

10. a cat's inherited _____ for hunting prey

MATCHING ANTONYMS

From the word list below, find an opposite for each numbered word and write it on the appropriate line.

traditionalist   kindle   deter   discord   elaborate

precipitate   peripheral   careless   spoken   honorable

1. unethical _____

2. central, main _____

3. douse _____

4. simple _____

5. harmony _____

6. encourage _____

7. tacit _____

8. considered _____

9. assiduous _____

10. iconoclast _____

MATCHING

In the group of words at the right, find two synonyms or phrases to write beside each of the words to the left.

1. scathing

_____

_____

2. propensity

_____

_____

3. peripheral

_____

_____

4. discord

_____

_____

5. tenuous

_____

_____

6. deter

_____

_____

7. insidious

_____

_____

8. paradigm

_____

_____

9. precipitate

_____

_____

10. assiduous

_____

_____

dangerously alluring

flimsy

lack of harmony

impetuous

discourage

model

caustic

strife

admired example

tendency

persistent

headlong

most attentive

inhibit

barely perceptible

auxiliary

highly critical

subtle

around the edge

inclination

Answers for this chapter begin on page 209.

A IS FOR ARBITRARY

---

arbitrary • blatant • capricious • desultory • extraneous • flagrant • devious • compatible • detrimental • susceptible • resigned • sporadic

---

ARBITRARY adj. *according to choice or impulse, rather than merit; in a tyrannical or despotic way*
I made an *arbitrary* decision to serve pizza at the class party. When there isn't a chance to consult a group or take a vote, I prefer to make an *arbitrary* choice and not worry about it.

BLATANT adj. *embarrassingly obvious, loud, or showy; brazen, tasteless*
Nobody likes to make a *blatant* error in public because it's embarrassing. Showing up in clothes that prove to be *blatantly* out of place, for instance, is pretty awkward.

CAPRICIOUS adj. *not steady, changing on a whim or "caprice"*
The stereotype of a female movie star is that of a *capricious* airhead. Actually, a good actress tries to be wholly professional and leaves *capricious* behavior to butterflies.

DESULTORY adj. *in a random, unplanned fashion; haphazard*
Last weekend we struck off into the woods on a long, *desultory* ramble that took us to a creek we'd never seen before. That's the fun of excursions done in a *desultory* way; you never know what you'll discover.

EXTRANEOUS adj. *extra, nonessential, irrelevant*
"No *extraneous* chitchat," said the guidance counselor as he blue-penciled my essay for college application. "Make a careful outline, then don't add even one *extraneous* word!"

HER/HES = to cling, stick

coherent—*logically arranged or ordered; lucid (clear)*
now *coherent* after the accident
a helpful, *coherent* talk

inherent—*natural, inborn, innate*
an *inherent* ability to swim
an *inherently* cheerful soul

Also: **adhere, adhesive, cohesive, incoherent, adherent**

FLAGRANT adj. *highly noticeable in a negative way; glaring*
Occasionally, Meatloaf goes for a stroll on the kitchen counters in *flagrant* disobedience of house rules. Cats are known for following their own interests, of course, no matter how *flagrant* their behavior.

DEVIOUS adj. *indirect, roundabout; cunning or deceptive; remote (as "a devious path through the woods")*
I can follow a trail, no matter how *devious*, but not the twists and turns of a *devious* mind. Perhaps the most infamous *devious* thinker was Nicolo Machiavelli; anything termed Machiavellian is noted for its cunning or duplicity.

COMPATIBLE adj. *well-suited; adaptable; related, similar*
Dogs and cats are supposed to be *incompatible*, but families with pets know better. A cat and dog raised together may be not only *compatible* but also very attached to one another. (Remember *The Incredible Journey*?)

CID/CIS = to cut; to kill

concise—*short and to the point; succinct; admirably brief*
a *concise*, effective speech
with delightful *conciseness*

incisive—*decisive, direct, and forceful in approach*
an *incisive* analysis
an *incisive* decision-maker

Also: **decide, decisive, incise, incision, excise, excision, precise, precision, homicide, fratricide, matricide**

DETRIMENTAL adj. *definitely harmful; damaging; pernicious*
Spraying hedgerows and ditches to kill weeds proved sadly *detrimental* to game birds like pheasants who lost their nesting sites. Modern ecologists know that we must stop any practice that is a *detriment* to our nation's wildlife.

SUSCEPTIBLE adj. *open to, subject to, or responsive to; impressionable; liable*
I tan easily, so I didn't believe I was *susceptible* to a bad sunburn. Wrong again, Ted. That same camp-out taught me that I had an extreme *susceptibility* to poison ivy, too.

RESIGNATION n. *acceptance of the inevitable or the obvious; submissiveness, surrender; formal notice of leaving a job or a responsibility*
Mom is finally *resigned* to the idea that I'll be working out of town this summer. "Your last summer at home," she said, with a sigh of weary *resignation*. "Parents *resign* themselves to the fact that kids grow and go—but it happens so fast."

SPORADIC adj. *occurring off and on; inconstant*
Dad said, "Ted'll be home *sporadically* over the summer." "You can count on me, Ma," I assured her. "It won't be *sporadic* either. I need to do laundry and eat real food at least every other weekend."

MEMORY FIX
Need we say it? Write them, stare at them, write their meanings, say them aloud.

SUBSTITUTION
Replace each italicized word or phrase with the correct word from this chapter.

1. You should consult all the club members, not just make a(n) *tryrannical* decision. _____

2. I was leafing through the anthology in a *random, unplanned* way when I found an incredible poem. _____

3. Spilling that after-shave lotion on my dresser was *extremely harmful* to the oak finish. _____

4. My mind must have wandered during the math test, because I made a *badly noticeable* error on an easy problem.

   _____

5. We may be *forced to face the inevitable* to our principal's leaving, but we don't have to like it. _____

6. I made some *off and on* attempts to pick up my room, but I got distracted and never finished. _____

7. The bee doesn't really flit in a(n) *unsteady, whimsical* way from flower to flower; she just looks disorganized.

   _____

8. Reggie's always advertising his store in such a *loud, embarrassingly pushy* way that I would never shop there.

   _____

9. It's tough to accept the idea of our *innately* imperfect nature until you watch toddlers push each other around.

   _____

10. Somebody should teach our manager how to deliver a(n) *decisively cutting to the heart of the matter* speech.

    _____

TRUE OR FALSE
Read each sentence to see how the words in this chapter are being used. Then mark **T** (true) or **F** (false) beside each.

1. If you wore a little asafetida bag the way kids did in "the old days," you wouldn't be *susceptible* to colds. _____

2. Teachers enjoy students who *flagrantly* flout school rules.

   _____

3. The Pony Express would have been more efficient if it had operated in a more *desultory* or *capricious* manner. _____

4. A landscaper with an inherently *devious* mind could prove to be a natural designer of garden mazes. _____

5. My painfully shy, withdrawn Aunt Willy would have communicated better with a more *incisive* psychologist. _____

6. Snakes and mice are naturally *compatible*. _____

MATCHING

Circle the two words or phrases that best explain the meaning of each word in bold type.

1. **coherent** sticky logical buddy lucid inaudible

2. **concise** succinct clear cohesive brief meager

3. **devious** putrid criminal roundabout unattractive crafty

4. **compatible** agreeable comfortable positive well-suited convivial

5. **susceptible** underdone ailing confused by liable receptive to

6. **extraneous** irrelevant nonessential critical central abundant

7. **inherent** hairless hirsute inborn basic natural

8. **blatant** delayed "loud" hereditary glaring stupid

9. **sporadic** moldy druggie topmost story irregular inconstant

10. **arbitrary** despotic mediating impulsive convenient selective

Answers for this chapter begin on page 209.

LISTS 21–25 REVIEW

The preceding five lists featured words you'll use for the rest of your life . . . and maybe on the SAT in a few weeks. Read each of those lists again to refresh your memory before completing this oh-so-helpful review.

ANALOGIES

Circle the one word pair in each list below that expresses the same relationship as the pair in capital letters.

1. **TIME : ANACHRONISTIC**
   - (A) era : mesozoic
   - (B) place : ubiquitous
   - (C) theory : hypothetical
   - (D) setting : incongruous
   - (E) country : utopian

2. **PROPHET : CLAIRVOYANT**
   - (A) tyrant : frugal
   - (B) paradigm : exemplary
   - (C) instructor : incisive
   - (D) architect : ethical
   - (E) iconoclast : vindictive

3. **APPARENT : FLAGRANT**
   - (A) brief : concise
   - (B) ubiquitous : omnipresent
   - (C) detrimental : harmful
   - (D) careful : assiduous
   - (E) sporadic : desultory

4. **WATER : TURBULENT**
   - (A) knowledge : esoteric
   - (B) excuse : extenuating
   - (C) decision : imprudent
   - (D) reason : unethical
   - (E) thought : incoherent

5. **APPETITE : VORACIOUS**
   - (A) milk : homogeneous
   - (B) apparel : voluminous
   - (C) mind : oblivious
   - (D) route : devious
   - (E) talent : minimal

6. **EXTRANEOUS : DETAIL**
   - (A) peripheral : issue
   - (B) animated : cartoon
   - (C) elusive : enigma
   - (D) generic : drug
   - (E) ingenuous : idea

FIND THE ODDBALL
In each word group, cross out the oddball, the one unrelated word or phrase.

1. genetic   gentleman   ingenious   brilliant   congenial

2. destiny   kismet   karma   predestination   fate   prophecy

3. conjectural   theoretical   hypothetical   pragmatic

4. fleeting   elusive   evasive   running   slippery

5. intending evil   malignant   swiftly powerful   virulent   hideous

6. unscathed   not touched   fragile   uninjured   harmful

7. spark   ignite   energize   elucidate   kindle   excite

8. alternate   discourage   inhibit   hinder   deter

9. erroneous   rash   impetuous   precipitate   headlong

10. indigent   brazen   tasteless   loud   blatant   showy

11. crooked   cunning   twisted   indirect   devious   inspired

12. forceful   direct   decisive   incisive   reclusive

WHO SAID THAT?
From the choices offered, select the type of speaker for each of the following comments.

> pragmatist   credulous one   clairvoyant   pious one
> eccentric   arbitrary one   iconoclast   vindictive one
> convivial soul

1. There, but for the grace of God, go I. _____

2. Oil paints are a silly tradition; I paint with mud. _____

3. You will go on a long journey. _____

4. How about a little dessert before dinner? _____

5. Why? Because I said so! (All parents are eventually driven to this, you know.) _____

6. Very sensible approach. I like it. _____

7. The ad promised I'd lose ten pounds in five days.

_____

8. I'll get you for that. _____

9. Yo, Goombah, let's party! _____

FIND THE SYNONYMS

From the word list below, choose two more synonyms to complete each group.

chimerical	frugal	propensity	desultory	tenuous
enigmatic	congenial	fanciful	parochial	cryptic
whimsical	thrifty	tendency	capricious	narrow
tacit	flimsy	compatible	haphazard	unspoken

1. like-minded _____   sociable _____

2. inconstant _____   fanciful _____

3. random _____   unplanned _____

4. obscure _____   mysterious _____

5. sparing _____   prudent _____

6. provincial _____   limited _____

7. insubstantial _____ slight _____

8. silent _____ understood _____

9. natural leaning _____ inclination _____

10. imaginary _____ improbable _____

THE ROOT OF IT ALL

Here's the root, with a blank for every missing letter and a definition for a clue.

1. _ _ **hes** _ _ _   gluey or sticky

2. **gen** _ _ _   brilliant person

3. _ _ **gen** _ _ _ _   innocent, naive, gullible

4. **gen** _   transmitter of hereditary factors

5. _ _ **gen** _ _ _   to foster, begin

6. **gen** _ _ _ _   of a general type or class

7. _ _ _ _ _ **gen** _ _ _ _   faking honesty

8. **cred** _ _ _ _   worthy of being believed

9. _ _ _ _ _ _ **ced** _   to mediate between disputants

10. **chron** _ _   habitual, long-lasting

11. **anim** _ _ _ _ _ _   bitter antagonism

12. _ _ _ **anim** _ _ _   of a balanced, even disposition

13. _ _ **sid** _ _ _ _   dangerously alluring; subtle

14. _ _ **ten** _ _ _ _ _ _   reducing in severity or importance

15. _ _ **cis** _ _ _   cutting teeth

Answers for this review lesson begin on page 210.

BOLSTER, DON'T CARP

exhaust • enervate • carp • coerce • bolster • belittle • advocate • cajole • facilitate • denounce • deplete • alienate

EXHAUST v. *to use up entirely; deplete; to wear out physically*
adj. **exhaustive**, *thorough*
Nothing is more *exhausting* than college applications. My brain *exhausted* all of its ideas for essays on the first few schools. Also, each form requires such an *exhaustive* roundup of information that it would *exhaust* anyone's patience.

ENERVATE v. *to drain of energy and mental quickness*
Totally *enervated* after spending hours on these applications, I sacked out for a little power nap. Filling in miles of forms had been *enervating* beyond belief.

CARP v. *to nag in a petty, nitpicky way; to find fault*
I woke up to hear Mom *carping* about the applications being due right now. "Hey, Ma," I said when I could get a word in, "don't *carp* at me. I'm working, I'm working!"

COERCE v. *to force or compel (someone or something)*
"We can't *coerce* you into hurrying," Mom said, "but it's so much smarter to turn the applications in early. Sorry about the nagging. *Coercion* isn't our style here, you know."

BOLSTER v. *to act as a support or prop; to reinforce*
I was feeling pretty sorry for myself, so I said, "Yeah, I need major *bolstering* right now, not criticism. Being a senior is tough; we all need to be *bolstered* now and then."

BELITTLE v. *to make fun of or reduce in importance; to disparage or decry*
"Oh, boo hoo," Mom said, grinning. "I hate to *belittle* your problems, but you could be worse off—such as not graduating and not going to college. Still, you'll never find me *belittling* the work those applications take."

CAP/CIP/CEPT = to take, get

incipient—*beginning to be; commencing*
    an *incipient* cold
    the *incipient* signs of spring

perceptive—*keenly observant; discerning; very understanding*
    my most *perceptive* friend
    a *perceptive* analysis

Also: **capture, captivate, caption, anticipate, reciprocate, emancipate, intercept, receptive, susceptible**

ADVOCATE v. *to support, recommend, be in favor of* n. *a person who pleads a case; lawyer*
Coming from Mom, who's always been my staunchest *advocate*, that was okay, but not terrific. However, she *advocates* total honesty within the family, and that's what I got.

CAJOLE v. *to beg earnestly, to wheedle or coax*
Hoping to *cajole* her into helping, I said, "I could really use just a teensy bit of—" and watched her shake her head. "No amount of *cajolery* will work this time. If you can't do the applications, you aren't ready for those schools."

FACILITATE v. *to make easier or simpler, to smooth the way*
"To *facilitate* your process," Mom suggested, "try using the school memories book that we've always kept. You'll get ideas from way back in kindergarten, and I'm sure that will *facilitate* the writing of all those essays."

FER = to carry, bear, bring

infer—*to conclude from available evidence; to deduce, guess*
    infer his meaning from his tone
    can *infer* when he's tired

proliferate—*to multiply, increase rapidly in number*
    cancerous cells that *proliferate*
    a *proliferation* of schools

Also: **confer, conference, vociferous, transfer, coniferous** *(cone-bearing)*, **proffer, offer, defer, deference**

DENOUNCE v. *to criticize, especially publicly; to accuse* n. **denunciation**, *negative criticism*

The record book was a great help, but inwardly I found myself *denouncing* college applications on all counts. It was a truly exhaustive *denunciation*; I didn't leave out any of the parts that I thought were most annoying.

DEPLETE v. *to greatly reduce any supply; to drain, bankrupt, or impoverish* n. **depletion**

By the time I finished all seven sets of forms, I had *depleted* my store of memories, my list of accomplishments, and my supply of good humor. My enthusiasm for going away to college had suffered some *depletion*, too, but it soon returned to bolster my spirits.

ALIENATE v. *to estrange, set apart by ill will (affections or people who had once been close)*

On discovering that I was one of the few who had finished all of his college applications, I kept quiet for fear of *alienating* my friends. Usually, I'd rather not mention something than *alienate* people.

MEMORY FIX
Once again, write each word you don't know, with a definition for each, then say the words aloud.

FILL IN THE BLANKS
From the new words in this chapter, select the one that best completes the meaning and logic of each sentence. Change the form of the word as required for correctness.

1. A long hike is _____ for the trained hiker only if some emergency forces him to _____ his energy early in the hike.

2. I don't mean to _____ your work, but picking up your room will probably not make the *Guinness Book of Records*.

3. Our family's tired of the constantly _____ critics on TV and in newspapers, who apparently never approve of anyone or anything.

4. We stayed with Amy until she went into surgery, hoping to
   _____ her spirits about losing her wisdom teeth.

5. "I can _____ from the look of your faces," she said,
   "that I'm not going to feel so hot when the anesthetic wears off."

6. Ever since she was little, Amy's been unusually
   _____ when it comes to reading faces.

7. General anesthesia drains me of energy for days afterward, so for
   me it has a seriously _____ effect.

8. In the dental recovery room, I could detect small bulges in Amy's
   cheeks, _____ signs of the swelling to come.

9. Hoping to _____ recovery by reducing swelling
   and pain, we held ice packs to Amy's cheeks.

10. No amount of _____ would have made Amy eat
    those first hours after surgery, but eventually we
    _____ her into drinking a milkshake.

ANTONYMS

You'll recognize some of these antonyms from past lists as you make the
match of opposites.

_____	1. bolster	acclaim
_____	2. deplete	energize
_____	3. denounce	dull, obtuse
_____	4. incipient	contain
_____	5. facilitate	undermine
_____	6. perceptive	extol
_____	7. enervate	terminal, final
_____	8. proliferate	hamper, hinder
_____	9. carp	replenish

SWITCHEROO

Many words in this lesson, in addition to being verbs, are also nouns and adjectives. Match these equally important words with their meanings.

_____	1. alienation	supporter
_____	2. advocacy	keenness
_____	3. depletion	conclusion, deduction
_____	4. perceptiveness	estrangement
_____	5. advocate	wheedling, begging
_____	6. proliferation	force
_____	7. inference	sponsorship, support
_____	8. denunciation	exhaustion
_____	9. cajolery	(rapid) multiplication
_____	10. coercion	negative criticism

Answers for this chapter begin on page 211.

**bizarre • prosaic • zany • static • urbane • opaque •
stoic • subtle • latent • innate • futile • candid**

BIZARRE adj. *strikingly unusual or incongruous; fantastic or
jolting in impact*
Our word *bizarre* was once *bizarro*, Spanish for "brave" or
"handsome," and also *bizar* for the Basques, who greatly admired
beards. Not the French; they loathed beards and termed the Basques
bizarre, meaning "strange."

PROSAIC adj. *ordinary, unexciting, dull, unimaginative*
I've led an awfully predictable, *prosaic* life so far. I'd like to do a year of
college studies abroad, which would be foreign and exciting, not at all
prosaic.

ZANY adj. *wacky, absurd, ludicrous, "crazy"*
Zany, a nickname for Giovanni (John), was a common way to address
servants in sixteenth-century Italy. In their local plays, a clowning
servant was a *Zani*, who always made a fool of his master. What a *zany*
history for a word!

STATIC adj. *unchanging; quiet, at rest; stationary, fixed;* n.
electronic noise; back talk (slang)
The last chem experiment concerned solutions that remained *static* in
spite of various attempts to destabilize them. When you think about it,
not much in life remains *static*.

URBANE adj. *smooth and sophisticated (said of men); suave*
From the Latin *urbs* (city) comes *urbane* to describe a polished city
fellow, the opposite of a country hick. Once, actor David Niven was
considered the epitome of the *urbane* male. (See the tape of *Around the
World in 80 Days*.)

ANTHROP = man, human being

misanthrope—*one who hates people or distrusts them*
    the attitudes of a confirmed *misanthrope*

philanthropy—*generous donation of time or money to benefit others (lit. love for human beings)*
    the famous *philanthropist* Andrew Carnegie

Also: **anthropoid, anthropology, anthropomorphism**

OPAQUE adj. *difficult to explain or to understand; mentally slow, obtuse, thick-skulled; also, not allowing light to pass through* n. **opacity**
The beautiful characters that make up the Chinese and the Japanese languages often appear daunting, even *opaque* to Westerners like me. I hate to think that I'm the one who's *opaque*, so I'll probably try to learn Japanese in college.

STOIC adj. *showing no feeling or pain; impassive*
Taking their name from the porch (*stoa*) where they met, the old Greek *Stoics* were taught by Zeno to be indifferent to passion or pain and to accept calmly whatever happened in life. People who could *stoically* ignore pain probably fared much better in ancient times.

AC/ACR = sharp

acute—*sharp or pointed; keenly perceptive (as "an acute eye")*
    an *acute* commentary
    family known for their *acute* minds

acrimonious—*bitterly sharp, rancorous, biting*
    an unusually *acrimonious* remark
    based on *acrimony*

exacerbate—*to make (a condition) worse; to aggravate*
    don't *exacerbate* that sprain
    illness *exacerbated* by worry

Also: **acrid, acrimony, acerbic, acumen** (All SAT favorites!)

SUBTLE adj. *not obvious in any way; elusive; hard to understand (as "a subtle language"); keenly discerning (as "subtle interpretation"); extremely clever; behaving in an insidious way (as "a subtle disease")*

Both cancer and AIDS are diseases feared for their *subtlety*. Scores of the country's *subtlest* medical minds are concentrated on these dreaded ailments.

LATENT adj. *hidden, submerged, waiting to be aroused or discovered; inactive, dormant, potential*

Throughout school, I kept hoping that good coaching would uncover a *latent* talent for some sport, preferably wrestling. But whatever I've got in the way of *latent* ability is still dormant, so now I'm looking for a sport that's just fun.

INNATE adj. *inborn, inherent, natural*

An *innately* talented composer, Mozart wrote music with skill and confidence before age 5. In the remaining thirty years of his life, he created over 600 compositions, many of which have an *innate* perfection of form that remains unmatched.

FUTILE adj. *ineffective, useless; vain (as "a futile hope")* n. futility (*Note:* utile = useful)

I've wasted a lot of time in *futile* tasks, such as trying to keep my room neat. I'm going to abandon this exercise in *futility*, because the room feels weird when it's too tidy.

CANDID adj. *honest, open, without guile or deceit; frank, even blunt* n. candor

Poet George Canning wrote, "Save, save, oh save me from the *candid* friend!" as a reminder that it's possible to be too frank with someone close to you. Sometimes a friend needs more thoughtfulness and a lot less *candor*.

MEMORY FIX

Here we go again. Write down each word you don't know; write its meaning, and say each one aloud.

TRUE OR FALSE

Read each sentence below to see how the new words in this chapter are being used. Then mark **T** (true) or **F** (false) beside each one.

  1. The best tone for a thank-you note is one of *acrimony*. _____

2. More rain will only *exacerbate* our current drought. _____

3. You'd better hope your dentist is not a *misanthrope.* _____

4. No one ever exhibits a trained rabbit, leading us to infer that bunnies are not overly *acute.* _____

5. "Mind over matter" is an apt motto for the *stoic.* _____

6. Many allegedly *futile* projects, such as going to the moon, have been accomplished; more will probably follow. _____

7. The opposite of misanthropy is *philanthropy.* _____

8. The caveman's stout club was proof of his innate *subtlety.* _____

9. Prepare to put on a *stoic* face if someone begins a conversation like this: "In all *candor* I feel I must tell you that. . . ." _____
_____

10. Chances are, everyone has *latent* abilities. _____

FIND THE SYNONYMS

From the word list below, add the correct synonyms to each numbered group by writing them on the appropriate lines.

dull-witted	inborn	guileless	suave	ordinary
unimaginative	insidious	shocking	potential	ludicrous
very clever	dormant	absurd	inherent	fantastic
sophisticated	obtuse	unchanging	frank	stationary

1. bizarre   incongruous   odd

_____   _____

2. prosaic   dull   humdrum

_____   _____

3. zany   wacko   crazy

_____   _____

4. static   fixed   quiet

_____   _____

5. urbane   polished   smooth

_____   _____

6. opaque   hard to penetrate or understand

_____   _____

7. subtle   elusive   very discerning

_____   _____

8. latent   hidden   inactive

_____   _____

9. innate   natural

_____   _____

10. candid   open   honest

_____   _____

SUBSTITUTION

For the words or phrases in italics, substitute the correct words from this chapter's word list.

1. There's nothing *dull or commonplace* about that checkout girl; it's an orangutan in a(n) *outlandish* costume.

_____   _____

2. He may be a(n) *polished*, well-dressed fellow, but under that designer haircut is an exceedingly *dim-witted* brain.

_____   _____

3. The *frank, open* comments of that hockey player with the *impervious to pain* look on his face led to a(n) *bitterly cutting* exchange. _____ _____

   _____

4. Don't give me any *negative noise* on that decision.

   _____

5. We've suggested that our *wacko* Aunt Jolly change her ways, but it's *useless* to even talk to her.

   _____ _____

Answers for this chapter begin on page 211.

LIST 28

NOT OBSOLETE AT ALL

---

quizzical • rigorous • reprehensible • salutary • prolific • recalcitrant • pedestrian • unassailable • volatile • superfluous • obsolete • diffident

---

QUIZZICAL adj. *teasing, but questioning too; puzzled*
"You're in charge of Senior Weekend?" Mom said with a *quizzical* look. "Tell me you're kidding!" Of course, I wasn't teasing, and her look went from *quizzical* to concerned.

RIGOROUS adj. *demanding or strict in requirements; absolutely accurate and precise; harsh (climate)*
"We'll expect you to keep *rigorous* accounts of all your expenses," the senior adviser told me. Any way I looked at it, I had taken on an extremely *rigorous* task.

REPREHENSIBLE adj. *deserving blame or criticism*
Then I had a *reprehensible* thought: What if I said I couldn't plan Senior Weekend after all? What was really *reprehensible* of me—and just plain dumb—was thinking that I could do this job without a committee of helpers.

SALUTARY adj. *promoting good health (mental or physical)*
The idea of helpers was so *salutary* that I cheered up and went in search of a committee. The five of us met over burgers and fries—tasty, though not very *salutary*—to discuss ideas for the weekend after graduation.

PROLIFIC adj. *very productive or fruitful; fertile, fecund*
Prolific critters such as mice and rabbits produce an impressive number of progeny. So do *prolific* minds create ideas; my committee suggested so many that we had trouble deciding what to do.

FLU/FLUX/FLUCT = to flow

mellifluous—*sweetly or smoothly flowing (of sounds or voices)*
  a *mellifluous* vocalist
  instrument with *mellifluous* tones

fluent—*gifted in speaking; graceful in movement; polished*
  a *fluent* speaker of French
  the *fluent* body of a gymnast

Also: **affluent, fluid, fluctuate, influence, confluence, effluent, effluvium, influx, flux, fluxion**

RECALCITRANT adj. *very tough to control; defiant of authority; unruly, refractory*
Four of us agreed on a great idea, but one *recalcitrant* kid said no. As I wondered how to win him over, I remembered that he'd been pretty stubborn and *recalcitrant* ever since kindergarten.

PEDESTRIAN adj. *commonplace, ordinary, unimaginative; referring to going by foot (as "a pedestrian walk")*
"Renting an old, broken-down camp for the weekend," Harold grumbled. "That's so ho-hum . . . so *pedestrian*! For once, can't we do something that isn't so boringly *pedestrian*?"

UNASSAILABLE adj. *not assailable; not open to attack, to question, or to doubt*
Jodie grinned. "Pedestrian, huh? Well, troops, we now have *unassailable* proof that Harold prepped for SATs." "Very funny," he retorted. "Also *unassailable* is the fact that we still haven't got a good idea!"

SPIC/SPEC/SPECT = to look, see

conspicuous—*very noticeable; commanding attention, striking*
  conspicuous by his absence
  a *conspicuous* display of talent

circumspect—*cautious, watchful, careful, and prudent*
  take the time needed for a *circumspect* decision

Also: **auspicious, suspicion, perspicacity, perspicuous, spectator, inspection, speculation, specious**

VOLATILE adj. *quick to express emotion; explosive, easily triggered (a chemical or a person's temper); changeable, unstable*
Now here's a *volatile* guy for you, I thought, wondering why I hadn't remembered Harold's quick temper. The other aspect of his *volatility*, however, was changeability, and as Jodie kept talking, Harold came around.

SUPERFLUOUS adj. *extra, unnecessary; or, wasteful*
Harold said, "Okay, just a few questions. First, and this is major, not *superfluous*, what are we going to do for two days? That camp barely has electricity, you know!" True, and electricity isn't exactly a *superfluous* item.

OBSOLETE adj. *out of date, not in use; outmoded, passé*
I'd forgotten that the camp's equipment was *obsolete*. Of course, I'd been thinking about the lake and the dock and the canoes, things that would never be *obsolete* for me.

DIFFIDENT adj. *hesitant, lacking confidence; unassertive*
"Well," I began *diffidently*, a new idea taking hold, "let's rough it, then. No electricity, no boom boxes—not one modern thing. Total nostalgia," I continued happily, my *diffident* attitude vanishing. "That wouldn't be pedestrian!"

MEMORY FIX
Of course you remember. Write the words you don't know with their definitions. Say them aloud and THINK.

FIND THE ODDBALL
In each word group, cross out the oddball, the one unrelated word or phrase.

1. proficient with language   fluent   skillful   articulate

2. dangerous   explosive   changeable   volatile   unstable

3. charming   smooth   richly flowing   mellifluous

4. unconfident   diffident   unsure   wary   unaggressive

5. hard to manage   pedestrian   naughty   defiant   unruly

MATCHING

In column B, find two synonyms or phrases that explain each word in
column A. Write them on the lines provided.

	A	**B**
_____	1. recalcitrant	prudent
_____		unnecessary
_____	2. circumspect	outmoded
_____		unimaginative
_____	3. diffident	refractory
_____		striking
_____	4. obsolete	totally accurate
_____		hesitant
_____	5. rigorous	productive
_____		fertile
_____	6. prolific	wasteful
_____		passé
_____	7. pedestrian	watchful
_____		demanding
_____	8. conspicuous	unassertive
_____		unruly
_____	9. superfluous	very noticeable
_____		ordinary

FILL IN THE BLANKS

Select the best word from this chapter's word list to complete the
meaning and logic of each sentence. Change any word as needed for
grammatical correctness.

1. Obviously puzzled as to my meaning, yet trying not to laugh, Jeff
    gave me a _____ glance and waited for my reply.

2. The pilot maintained he could fly anything, even the most
    _____ propeller plane in the hangar.

3. As a result of the massive data compiled during that study, their conclusions are virtually _____.

4. A brisk walk is one traditional way of starting the day in a _____ way.

5. For the person who's done something _____, there's an old saying: "Confession is good for the soul."

6. Valiant soldiers are decorated for _____ bravery.

7. A typical European, _____ in at least two or three languages, puts most Americans to shame.

8. _____ outdoor programs like Outward Bound have proved to be effective at building self-esteem.

9. Janie's is the sweetest voice on earth, the only _____ one in the midst of that cacophony of noise.

10. A moody, _____ person is apt to erupt like Pinatubo.

Answers for this chapter begin on page 211.

---

aloof • partisan • demeanor • altruism • austere •
provincial • authoritarian • nonchalant • brusque •
contrite • conciliatory • spurious

ALOOF adj. *reserved or cool in manner; uninvolved, remote*
Nearly 200 years ago, Coleridge wrote: "*Aloof* with hermit-eye I scan / The present works of present man— / A wild and dreamlike trade of blood and guile, / Too foolish for a tear, too wicked for a smile." Looks as if it's always been tough to remain *aloof* from the evil that people keep creating.

PARTISAN adj. *strongly in favor, biased, prejudiced* n. *follower or member*
In a country tired of *partisan* politics, the American electorate hungers for representatives who will put the good of the country, not their political party, first. Many voters feel that pure *partisan* voting is blind voting.

DEMEANOR n. *manner of handling yourself; mien, comportment, bearing*
Queens are often described as having a stately *demeanor*, and busy officials have a bustling *demeanor*. Our *demeanor* is our body language and a major clue to character.

ALTRUISM n. *unselfish giving for the benefit of others* Society has some full-time *altruists*, like teaching nuns and priests or Peace Corps volunteers, and now and then the rest of us are motivated by *altruism*. Major religions are based on the *altruistic* concept that those who give will receive.

AUSTERE adj. *reserved, grave, somber in manner; self-denying, abstemious; restrained* n. **austerity**
People who devote their lives to others aren't self-indulgent, so the altruistic life is often quite *austere*. One example of holy *austerity* is that of the contemplative monks who work and mediate in silence, talking only rarely.

FID = faith

infidel—*a disbeliever in some specific sense*
  declared him an *infidel* and banned him from the church

perfidy—*faithlessness, disloyalty; betrayal, treachery*
  hated for his *perfidy*
  what *perfidious* behavior

Also: **confide, confidence, fidelity, diffident, diffidence, affidavit, confidant** *(intimate, trusted friend)*

PROVINCIAL adj. *referring to the provinces, or country; unsophisticated; or, parochial, narrow* n. **provincial**
Abraham Lincoln was once scorned as a *provincial* fellow by those who equated sophistication with intelligence. That same error was made by the city mouse who thought his country cousin was a *provincial*.

AUTHORITARIAN adj. *favoring subservience or allegiance to an authority rather than personal independence or freedom*
Author Edmund Wilson said, "Marx and Engels, coming out of *authoritarian* Germany, tended to imagine socialism in *authoritarian* terms." Independent Americans, of course, are never very comfortable with *authoritarian* governments.

NONCHALANT adj. *casual, carefree, cool, unconcerned*
Nonchalant at first, our family shrugged and said, "Oh, well, we can probably live with a few bats in the attic." But that *nonchalance* vanished when we began to smell something.

ERR = to wander

erratic—*on no set course, wandering, nomadic; devious*
  the *erratic* path of the butterfly
  at *erratic* intervals

aberration—*eccentricity; an oddity, not the norm*
  signs of an *aberrant* mind
  the *aberrations* of a recluse

Also: **error, erroneous, errant, arrant** *(extreme)*

BRUSQUE adj. *curt, abrupt, blunt (unpleasant in effect)*
When I said I needed to get rid of some bats in our attic, the clerk at the bat and bird shop snapped *brusquely*, "You should appreciate bats." Put off by her *brusque* manner, I said I was crazy about them, but not in my house.

CONTRITE adj. *sorrowful or repentant for some wrong* n. **contrition**
We're going to evict the bats from our house if we can, and we will not feel *contrite*. Well, maybe we'll suffer a few momentary pangs of *contrition*, but the bats can move to a nearby belfry.

CONCILIATORY adj. *reconciling, appeasing, pacifying (to improve relations)* v. **conciliate**
As a *conciliatory* gesture to the bats, I opened the louvers on the belfry of our church, advertising its desirability as a bat residence. I don't mind *conciliating* bats, who consume zillions of annoying bugs and mosquitoes.

SPURIOUS adj. *false, fake, though appearing legitimate; forged (as "a spurious passport")*
Opening the louvers to promote our church belfry as a home for the bats was not *spurious* advertising, because bats have always liked belfries. Generally speaking, though, the world of advertising generates a fair number of *spurious* claims.

MEMORY FIX
Very near the end now. . . . Write down each word you don't know well; write definitions for each. Say them aloud.

FILL IN THE BLANKS
From the new words in this chapter, select the one that best completes the meaning and logic of each phrase. Use the correct form of each word.

1. moved with the regal _____ of a Paris model

2. tossed his head _____ as if it didn't matter to him

3. ordered us to leave in a most _____ manner

4. Vidkun Quisling, a traitor whose _____ resulted in his surname becoming a word

5. following the wild, _____ path of the fleeing rabbit

6. apologizing for the omission with a sincere, _____ smile

7. illegal immigrants entering the United States with _____ documents

8. made timid by her _____, forbidding countenance

9. a generous person, known for a life of _____

10. eager to make up, extending his hand in a _____ gesture

WHO SAID THAT?

From the list below, choose the most likely speaker to go with each remark.

an infidel	a partisan	the brusque type
the provincial	the authoritarian	an austere person
an altruist	a perfidious one	a nonchalant one

1. I have no need of jewelry or stylish clothes or elegantly prepared foods. The simple life suits me. _____

2. We don't have to deal with that out here where there's a mile between neighbors, you see? _____

3. Briefly, that's it. Don't get it? Tough. _____

4. I am my brother's keeper. _____

5. They aren't like us—not at all, no sir. Why they should be so different from us is beyond me. _____

6. I'm not wearing that thing over my face and walking meekly behind him; you can just forget it! _____

7. Just do what I said and don't ask questions.

_____

8. I leaked that information, and I'd do it again.

_____

9. No sweat. Don't let it bother you. _____

TRUE OR FALSE

Read each sentence to see how the new words in this chapter are being used. Then mark **T** (true) or **F** (false) beside each one.

1. To Americans, cannibalism is more than a mere *aberration*.

_____

2. For the sake of our teachers, we should turn in assignments on an *erratic* basis. _____

3. Neutral nations avoid entanglements, remaining *aloof*. _____

4. After bopping your brother on the head, you should assume a *contrite demeanor* and apologize. _____

5. The psychologist who masters a *brusque* approach will be the most successful. _____

6. One of the better *conciliatory* lines is, "We'll make sure that doesn't happen again." _____

7. To think that only private schools can offer a good education is a *provincial* outlook. _____

8. A *bipartisan* committee will probably write the Republican platform for the next election. _____

Answers for this chapter begin on page 212.

ON THE DARK SIDE

---

negligence • deleterious • depravity • crass • morose •
caustic • guile • clandestine • cynical • furtive •
apprehension • decadence

NEGLIGENCE n. *lack of a sensible amount of care; neglect, carelessness* adj. **negligent**
Having bats in your house is not a sign of *negligence*, as bats can enter through the tiniest of openings. Learning that we hadn't been *negligent* homeowners helped us to feel somewhat better about the bats in our attic.

DELETERIOUS adj. *causing harm or injury, maybe in a very subtle way; maybe pernicious (deadly)*
We began to fret about the *deleterious* effects the bats might have on our house. One especially *deleterious* result of their invasion was the steady accumulation of bat guano.

DEPRAVITY n. *a state of corruption, perversion, or evil* adj. **depraved**
Grinning, Dad said, "I suggest we bag that stuff and sell it for fertilizer . . . if you don't think that's too *depraved*." Hearing our quite well-mannered father link himself to *depravity* made us hoot with laughter.

CRASS adj. *utterly lacking in taste or discrimination*
"I hate to sound *crass*," Mom interrupted, "but what do you think we could get for a bag of bat poo?" Coming from her, that was a *crass* remark, all right, but awfully funny.

MOROSE adj. *very gloomy or sullen in manner*
Amy stared *morosely* at the floor. Finally she said, "Look at me, troops. This is a depressed person wearing a *morose* face because we've got a real problem and you're all acting wacko!"

BEL/BELL = war

belligerent—*combative, liking to start fights, bellicose*
    a *belligerent* attitude
    historically *belligerent* nations

rebellious—*resisting or opposing authority, refractory, recalcitrant*
    a *rebellious* attitude that always led to trouble

Also: **rebel, rebellion, antebellum** *(before the Civil War)* [And also **bell** = beauty—*belle, embellish*]

CAUSTIC adj. *biting, incisive, cutting, corrosive*
That was a pretty *caustic* approach for Amy, but her bedroom is right under the bats' roosting area. I guess I'd have a few *caustic* comments myself if my room were that close to the bat colony.

GUILE n. *trickery or deceit; deceptive cunning; duplicity*
Eventually, our family agreed that, although we liked bats and benefited from their insect-eating prowess, we would use every bit of *guile* we had to evict them. No strangers to cunning, bats are *guileful* creatures themselves at times.

CLANDESTINE adj. *secret, surreptitious*
Of course, I had already made a *clandestine* trip to our church belfry to open the louvres wider, hoping to lure the bats into the belfry. I'd been deliberately *clandestine* about my mission at church, because it sounded weird.

VERS/VERT = to turn

diverge—*to alter a course; to go apart from one point; to differ in opinion; to deviate; to swerve*
        diverging rays of sunlight
        attitude *diverged* from the norm

diverse—*unlike, different*
        went their *diverse* ways
        several *diverse* opinions on that

Also: **revert, overt, covert, versatile, inadvertant, divert, diversion, perverse, controversy, extrovert, introvert**

CYNICAL adj. *distrustful of human nature; pessimistic, even misanthropic*

"I hate to be *cynical*," Dad said, "but how do you know that our bats will want to move to a belfry?" Of course I didn't know, and I was having deeply *cynical* thoughts myself about our ability to convince the bats to move out.

FURTIVE adj. *on the sly, in secret; surreptitious; stolen*

I zipped upstairs for a *furtive* peek at my old encyclopedia. Reading those basic bat facts again gave me an idea. There would be another *furtive* trip, I decided, this time to the bats' attic home, with an ultrasound device in hand.

APPREHENSION n. *a foreboding of something bad; or, legal arrest*

Wishing I felt less *apprehension*, I prayed that the bats would move away from the electronic jamming of their radar. And what if they didn't? I waited *apprehensively* for the worst—Dad's call to an exterminator—but bats are smart, and ours soon moved next door to the belfry.

DECADENCE n. *decline and decay; deterioration*

We didn't have a totally *decadent* party after the bats left; I mean, we didn't really fall apart, but it was a loud, late party. Our neighbors made some not-too-subtle comments about how noisy it must have been in old, *decadent* Rome.

MEMORY FIX

For the last time! Write down each word you don't know well along with a definition for each. Say them aloud.

WORDS IN CONTEXT

Write the meanings of the words in italics on the lines provided.

1. Arranging a *clandestine* meeting with the current love of your life is okay, but if you plan a *furtive* meeting, I'll be *apprehensive*, because *furtive* has more negative connotations.

    _____   _____

    _____   _____

2. It's no surprise to learn that a *depraved* lifestyle has *deleterious* effects on health. _____   _____

3. History tells us that the *decadence* of Rome led to its decline.

    _____

4. Stung by several of his *caustic* remarks, I belatedly reminded myself that the fellow was a well-known *cynic*.

    _____   _____

5. Although Americans are obviously obsessed with money, it is considered by some to be a *crass* topic. _____

6. Is there such a thing as a purely *guileless* soul? _____

7. Mouth set in a *rebellious* pout, he remained silent.

    _____

8. After I accused him of gross *negligence*, he turned to me and sneered *morosely*, "So what?"

    _____   _____

MATCHING SYNONYMS

Match the words in column A with their synonyms or definitions in column B.

	A	B
_____	1. clandestine	in poor taste
_____	2. diverge	foreboding
_____	3. caustic	deterioration
_____	4. diverse	pessimistic
_____	5. apprehension	deceit
_____	6. decadence	secret
_____	7. crass	biting, corrosive
_____	8. belligerent/ bellicose	to go apart
_____	9. guile	different
_____	10. cynical	spoiling for a fight

RHYME TIME

Add what is needed from this chapter's list of words to these varied bits of poetry, some wonderful, some corny.

1. The English teacher's face was long and _____.
   "Oh why," she cried, "are my writers verbose?"

2. "Macavity, Macavity, there's no one like Macavity,
   For he's a fiend in feline shape, a monster of
   _____."
   From *Old Possum's Book of Practical Cats,* T. S. Eliot

3. Cartoon cat Tom assumes a(n) _____ air,
   And we know he's tiptoeing toward Jerry's lair.

4. He said, "Let me at him," with a(n) _____ grin,
   Laced up his boxing gloves and waded in.

5. "Two roads _____ in a yellow wood," begins
   one of the most famous pieces of poetry ever written, by Robert
   Frost. Beginning at one place, the two roads followed a different
   path, and Frost "took the one less traveled by." Remember?

Answers for this chapter begin on page 212.

LISTS 26–30 REVIEW

Yahoo, the last review! Read each group of words in lists 26 to 30 aloud and think of what each word means. Now you're ready for this final review.

ANALOGIES

Circle the one word pair in each list below that expresses the same relationship as the pair in capital letters.

1. **DOCUMENT : SPURIOUS**
   (A) flight : erratic
   (B) nation : decadent
   (C) outline : diverse
   (D) passport : false
   (E) effort : futile

2. **RESOURCES : DEPLETE**
   (A) supplies : facilitate
   (B) health : enervate
   (C) strength : exhaust
   (D) force : coerce
   (E) energy : assail

3. **CARPING : ALIENATION**
   (A) apprehension : foreboding
   (B) perfidy : aberration
   (C) acrimony : conciliation
   (D) partisanship : rebellion
   (E) negligence : decadence

4. **MISANTHROPE : CYNICAL**
   (A) pedestrian : obsolete
   (B) stoic : impassive
   (C) altruist : unassailable
   (D) philanthropist : nonchalant
   (E) zany : depraved

5. **SUBTLE : COVERT**
   (A) flagrant : conspicuous
   (B) latent : innate
   (C) furtive : crass
   (D) reprehensible : bizarre
   (E) austere : provincial

6. **PARTISAN : ALOOF**
   (A) judge : perceptive
   (B) infidel : loyal
   (C) rebel : affluent
   (D) colonel : rigorous
   (E) buyer : urbane

MATCHING ANTONYMS

Match the words in column A with their opposites in column B.

	A	B
_____	1. reprehensible	deleterious
_____	2. urbane	belittle
_____	3. candid	learned, acquired
_____	4. bolster	docile
_____	5. salutary	vital
_____	6. recalcitrant	laudable
_____	7. innate	conciliatory
_____	8. austerity	self-absorption
_____	9. superfluous	coerce
_____	10. acrimonious	provincial
_____	11. cajole	guileful
_____	12. altruism	self-indulgence

MATCHING

Circle the two words or phrases that best explain the meaning of each numbered word in bold type.

1. **fluent**
   orally skilled   verbose   swiftly flowing   graceful   polite

2. **latent**
   delayed   recent   potential   dormant   lost

3. **diffident**
   unassertive   strange   unusual   hesitant   argumentative

4. **contrite**
   boring   banal   remorseful   repentant   angry

5. **crass**
   gross   mean-spirited   tasteless   thoughtless   grasping

6. **furtive**

surreptitious   illegal   superstitious   clandestine   forbidden

7. **acute**

perceptive   charming   geometric   pointed   painful

8. **infer**

popular pine tree   conclude   resume   deduce   suppose

9. **prosaic**

pedestrian   enervating   tiring   everyday   unpoetic

10. **authoritarian**

democratic   autocratic   despotic   rigorous   demonic

FILL IN THE BLANKS

From the list below, select the best word to complete each sentence. Alter the words as required for grammatical correctness.

erratic   static   facilitate   aberration   caustic
advocate   diverse   rigorous   circumspect   prolific
morose   denounce   futile   bellicose

1. Trained as a biochemist, Isaac Asimov was one of our century's most versatile, _____ authors, publishing over 300 books on _____ topics.

2. The dynamics of a changing community assure that almost nothing within it will remain _____ for long.

3. Can anything be done to _____ the use of high-speed rail in this country, or is that a _____ cause, doomed to fail?

4. "I'm afraid the old dog's _____ heartbeat is the norm for him now, not just a temporary _____," said the vet.

5. It's one thing to be _____, but Mother's Aunt Aggie is so unswervingly prudent that she never has any fun.

6. You can wipe that _____, down-in-the-mouth look off your face with some _____ exercise that enlivens mind and body.

7. Always quick to criticize, the media have enjoyed _____ the new administration with one _____ comment after another.

8. Some boys have such a _____ nature that counselors _____ sports like boxing to help them vent their aggression.

TRUE OR FALSE

Read the sentences below to see if the words in the past five chapters are being used correctly. Then mark **T** (true) or **F** (false) beside each one.

1. Someone exhibiting a *nonchalant demeanor* in the presence of highly *volatile* substances manipulated by a *zany* fanatic can indeed be characterized as cool. _____

2. It helps if the instructions to your VCR are somewhat *opaque*. _____

3. *Proliferation* of nuclear weapons *exacerbates* an already *apprehensive* attitude on the part of many. _____

4. You can be *enervated* even by an *incipient* illness. _____

5. You're apt to give a *bizarre* outfit a *quizzical* look. _____

6. *Brusque* funeral home directors do a thriving business. _____

Answers for this review lesson begin on page 213.

THE ANSWERS

WHAT YOU ALREADY KNOW—A QUICK REVIEW

Lesson A, Memory Check (p. 10)

Prefix A/AN; Meaning: *not, without*; Examples: atheist, anomaly, atypical

Prefix AB/ABS; Meaning: *from, away*; Examples: absent, abdicate, abstain

Prefix DIS/DI/DIFF; Meaning: *away, apart, negative*; Examples: disparate, dissuade, difference

Prefix ANTE/ANTI; Meaning: *before, previous*; Examples: anteroom, anticipate

Prefix BENE; Meaning: *good, well*; Examples: benefit, benevolent, beneficial

Prefix CIRCU; Meaning: *around*; Examples: circumference, circumvent, circuit

Prefix DI/DIA; Meaning: *across, apart, through*; Examples: diameter, dialogue, dilate

Prefix ANTI; Meaning: *against, opposing*; Examples: antisocial, antidote, antipathy

Prefix CO/COL/COM; Meaning: *with, together*; Examples: cooperate, concede, concur

Lesson B, Memory Check 1 (p. 12)

1. outside 2. mixed, not all the same 3. *in*decent and *in*substantial 4. playing it for all you're worth, to the *max*imum 5. bad; *maleficent* literally means *make bad* 6. changes or alters

Lesson B, Memory Check 2 (p. 14)

Prefix MICRO; Meaning: *small*; Examples: microbe, microphone, microcosm

Prefix PRE; Meaning: *before*; Examples: predict, prefix, preliminary

Prefix ORTH; Meaning: *straight, right*; Examples: orthopedic, orthodox

Prefix PER; Meaning: *through, throughout*, or *completely, wrongly*; Examples: permeate, permit

Prefix PERI; Meaning: *around, near*; Examples: periscope, perimeter, periphery

Prefix PRO; Meaning: *for, forward, before, forth, favoring*; Examples: promote, provision

Prefix POST; Meaning: *after, following*; Examples: postpone, postmortem, posterior

Prefix RE/RETRO; Meaning: *back, again*; Examples: recoil, retreat, retroactive

Prefix OMNI/PAN; Meaning: *all, entire*; Examples: omnipresent, pantheon, pandemic

Lesson B, Memory Check 3 (p. 16)

1. *se*parated 2. afar 3. *sub*marine 4. Super, super, *sur*pass 5. *syn*chronizing, together

LIST 1 (p. 17)

Fill In the Blanks

1. acquiese 2. condone 3. effaced 4. chastise 5. concurred 6. laud 7. amass
8. augment 9. digress 10. cursory 11. digressive 12. coalesced 13. disperse
14. disperse 15. emitted

Analogies

1. (C) chastise : misbehavior :: laud : success

   Implied comparison. Behaviors linked to the verbs most commonly associated with them.

2. (E) footprints : efface :: record : obliterate

   Implied comparison. Two human traces and ways in which they are commonly "wiped out," completely eradicated.

3. (B) acquiese : yielding :: disperse : scattering

   Inherent linkage. *Acquiesce* always implies giving way or yielding, just as *disperse* always refers to scattering in some sense.

4. (A) path : stray :: lecture : digress

   Implied comparison. To leave a path is to *stray* off it, just as leaving the main point of a lecture is to *digress*. These words are linked by usage as well as by meaning.

5. (C) pardon : offense :: condone : error

   Implied comparison. An *offense*, if excused, is said to be *pardoned*, whereas an *error*—less serious in nature—is said to be *condoned* if someone overlooks it or makes excuses.

Matching

1. (B) assent, (D) yield 2. (A) utter, (B) voice 3. (B) chastise, (C) scold
4. (A) forerunner, (D) harbinger 5. (B) accumulate, (C) gather 6. (A) enlarge,
(B) add to 7. (B) strew around, (D) disseminate 8. (A) join, (C) come together
9. (B) wear away, (C) erase 10. (A) sketchy, (D) hasty

LIST 2 (p. 23)

True or False

1. F 2. T 3. F 4. F 5. T 6. F 7. T 8. F 9. T 10. T

Matching

1. d 2. g 3. l 4. h 5. i 6. c 7. e 8. k 9. a 10. j 11. b 12. f

Fill In the Blanks

1. banal and hackneyed (and maybe also trite and full of platitudes!) 2. concise, succinct, laconic, terse, and pithy 3. hyperbole 4. platitude, banality 5. equivocal

LIST 3 (p. 28)
Fill In the Blanks

1. insurgents 2. hypocritical 3. hedonistic 4. glutton 5. inexorable 6. charlatans (possibly hypocrites or sycophants) 7. skeptical 8. despot 9. heretic 10. zealot 11. miser 12. bigoted 13. sycophant 14. verify

Rhyme Time

1. Gluttony (Yes, Orson Welles really said this.) 2. fanatic 3. oracle 4. skeptic 5. sycophant 6. hedonist 7. inexorable 8. aver

Matching

1. (m) Scrooge, (c) hoarder 2. (d) nonbeliever, (p) one who differs 3. (f) tyrant, (h) autocrat 4. (i) fake, fraud; (g) impostor 5. (a) bias, (k) prejudice 6. (o) confirm, (b) corroborate 7. (l) fanatical, (n) overeager 8. (j) one in revolt, (e) rebel

LIST 4 (p. 33)
Fill In the Blanks

1. superficiality 2. listlessness 3. fervor 4. profusion 5. vulnerability 6. indulgence 7. unobtrusiveness 8. uniformity

True or False

1. T 2. F 3. F 4. T 5. T 6. T 7. T 8. T 9. F 10. T

Matching Antonyms

1. (a) irrelevant, (m) inappropriate 2. (d) restrained, (n) stingy 3. (e) inconsistent, (p) varied 4. (f) exhilarating, (k) restful 5. (g) thorough, (l) deeply serious 6. (b) weak, (q) ineffective 7. (j) critical, (o) unforgiving (maybe also n. stingy) 8. (h) bouncy, (s) enthusiastic 9. (i) gregarious, (r) friendly 10. (t) conspicuous, (c) aggressive

LIST 5 (p. 38)
Matching

1. (B) exceedingly particular, (C) meticulous 2. (C) disapprove of, (D) regret 3. (A) prideful, (D) overbearing 4. (A) stoop, (B) unbend 5. (B) scorn, (C) disdain 6. (C) belittle, (D) mock or jeer 7. (A) smug, (B) self-satisfied 8. (B) privilege, (D) right 9. (A) scoff at, (C) ridicule 10. (B) minimize, (C) decry

Words in Context

1. openly and disdainfully proud 2. showy, self-important, pompous 3. disdainfully superior, scornful, proud 4. scorn, contempt 5. scorned, strongly disapproved of 6. scornful, disparaging, belittling, negatively critical 7. snootily and rather scornfully coming down to another's level (may be very subtle or quite open) 8. right, privilege 9. an "Oh, don't mind me" attitude that is modest and self-effacing, intended to put that person in the background 10. smugness, self-satisfaction

Analogies

1. (D) Napoleon : arrogance :: Twain : satire

   Person linked to well-known skill or trait.

2. (B) remark : disparaging :: attitude : scoffing

   Implied comparison. A remark that puts another down is a *disparaging* remark, just as an attitude that puts another down is *scoffing*.

3. (D) pride : hauteur :: satisfaction : complacency

   Escalating degree. Extreme pride is *hauteur* just as the extreme of satisfaction is *complacency*.

4. (E) derision : ridicule :: scorn : contempt

   Analogy of definition or main characteristic. *Derision* always involves or means *ridicule*, just as *scorn* implies *contempt* (by definition).

REVIEW, LISTS 1–5

Find the Oddball

1. heretic 2. hauteur 3. insist 4. nasty 5. hyperbole 6. interesting 7. provoke 8. inevitable 9. hedonist 10. hackneyed

True or False

1. T 2. F 3. F 4. F 5. F 6. F 7. T 8. T 9. T 10. F

Find the Synonym

1. equivocal 2. to concur 3. banal 4. listless 5. to chastise 6. charlatan 7. to condone 8. precursor 9. inexorable 10. grueling 11. profuse 12. potent

Who Said That?

1. orator 2. raconteur 3. glutton 4. recluse 5. skeptic 6. despot 7. insurgent 8. scoffer 9. heretic 10. equivocator 11. interrogator 12. deprecator

Matching

1. to come together 2. to praise 3. superficial or hasty 4. pompous language 5. banality 6. to declare firmly 7. accidental 8. to ridicule 9. right or privilege 10. disdain, scorn 11. to increase 12. to scatter or fan out 13. to obliterate; wear away 14. lenient 15. continuous

LIST 6 (p. 48)

Rhyme Time

1. raze 2. immutable 3. posit 4. meander 5. mutant

Matching

1. (A) blemish, (C) spoil 2. (C) relieve, (D) alleviate 3. (B) efface, (C) wipe out 4. (A) snub, (D) reject 5. (B) collect, (D) accumulate 6. (A) cloud over, (B) conceal 7. (C) study carefully, (D) examine 8. (B) wander, (C) ramble 9. (C) soothe, (D) appease 10. (B) tear down, (D) demolish 11. (A) invalidate, (D) negate 12. (B) mind or obey, (C) consider

Substitution

1. heed 2. proponent 3. marred 4. obscured 5. mitigate 6. rebuffed 7. placate 8. perusing 9. nullify 10. garnered

LIST 7 (p. 53)

Fill In the Blanks

1. virtuosos or virtuosi 2. quandary 3. lucid 4. parsimonious 5. zenith 6. Torpor 7. nostalgia 8. volition 9. reticent 10. temerity

Matching Antonyms

1. confidence 2. bombast 3. nadir 4. hyperactive 5. timidity 6. to obscure 7. order 8. beginner 9. descendant 10. generosity

Find the Oddball

1. assortment 2. angle 3. niece 4. instinct 5. temperament 6. quest 7. betrayal 8. transparent 9. fear 10. quaintness

LIST 8 (p. 58)

Find the Synonym

1. formidable 2. profound 3. untenable 4. tenet 5. resilient 6. astute 7. meticulous 8. tenacious 9. alleviate

True or False

1. F 2. T 3. F 4. T 5. T 6. F 7. T 8. T 9. T 10. F 11. F

Analogies

1. (C) lawyer : astute :: pathologist : painstaking

   Person linked to most desirable trait.

2. (D) profound : thoughtful :: sagacious : bright

   Descending degree. *Profound* is very deeply thoughtful just as *sagacious* is exceedingly bright.

3. (D) Supreme Court : sagacity :: muscles : resilience

   Noun linked to most critical quality, one that is the defining factor.

4. (E) formidable : defense :: redoubtable : warrior

   Noun linked to logical adjective. The best kind of defense is *formidable*, just as the best warrior is *redoubtable*.

LIST 9 (p. 63)

Word Analysis

1. good or mellow, jangly or jarring noise 2. optimist, pessimist 3. stringent, lax 4. Objective, subjective 5. concrete, abstract 6. burgeon, atrophy 7. affluent, indigent 8. levity, gravity 9. consecrated, desecrates 10. irrefutable, refuted 11. irresolute, resolute

Using the Words

1. atrophy, burgeon 2. irrefutable, refutable 3. objective, subjective 4. desecrate, consecrate 5. abstract, concrete 6. lax, stringent 7. cacophony, euphony 8. optimism, pessimism 9. gravity, levity 10. resolute, irresolute

LIST 10 (p. 69)

Fill In the Blanks

1. irascible 2. rancor (perhaps rue or malice) 3. premonition 4. surreptitiously 5. tawdry 6. sullen 7. writhing 8. malice (rancor) 9. taciturn 10. servile 11. malice 12. rue

Matching

1. self-reproach, guilty unease 2. forewarning, foreboding 3. slander, defame 4. quietly resentful, lowering 5. bitterness, old enmity 6. cheap, gaudy 7. secretive, deceptive 8. laconic, silent 9. subservient, abject 10. testy, choleric

Rhyme Time

1. writhe 2. rue 3. admonished 4. malice 5. mediocre 6. mediate

REVIEW, LISTS 6–10

Find the Synonym

1. obscure 2. mitigate 3. immutable 4. respite 5. parsimonious 6. lucid 7. astute
8. abstract 9. burgeon 10. resolute 11. sacrilege 12. taciturn

Analogies

1. (D) symphony : violins :: religion : tenets

Part of a whole. Violins are a significant part of any *symphony*, just as various *tenets* are part of any religion.

2. (B) energy : torpor :: government : anarchy

Opposites. Also, think of this sentence: Lacking energy, you have *torpor*; lacking government, you have *anarchy*.

3. (B) sin : remorseful :: mistake : rueful

Implied comparison. If you commit a sin you feel *remorseful*, just as making a mistake causes you to feel *rueful*.

4. (E) past : nostalgia :: future : optimism

Implied comparison. We typically view the past with *nostalgia*, just as we view the future with *optimism*. (C) is a weak choice because not everyone views the present with pessimism.

5. (C) mediate : sage :: elucidate : teacher

Specific person linked to one major function inherent in that position. A sage is well qualified to *mediate*, just as a teacher is well qualified to *elucidate*.

6. (C) battle : trepidation :: enemy : rancor

Implied comparison. We typically view a battle with *trepidation* just as we view an enemy with *rancor*.

Matching Antonyms

1. heir 2. indigent 3. levity 4. lax 5. rigidity 6. malicious 7. irritate 8. scan
9. ignore 10. temerity 11. silly 12. even-tempered

Fill In the Blanks

1. garner 2. meticulous 3. reticent 4. rebuffed 5. razed, obliterating 6. volition
7. quandary 8. irrefutable 9. proponents 10. virtuosos 11. tenacious 12. zenith

LIST 11 (p. 78)

Substitution

1. rejuvenate 2. vacillating 3. implying 4. temper 5. acclaim 6. venerate or revere
7. scrutinized 8. disclaim 9. sanctions, sanction (v.) 10. waived

Find the Oddball

1. sponge 2. twist 3. flinch 4. dankness 5. implied 6. deter 7. urge 8. discourage
9. relegate 10. reject

True or False

1. F 2. T 3. T 4. T 5. T 6. F 7. F 8. T

LIST 12 (p. 83)

Fill In the Blanks

1. criteria 2. delineate 3. dearth, prodigious (or copious) 4. minced
5. magnanimously

Matching

1. (B) briefness, (D) conciseness 2. (C) outline, (D) portray accurately 3. (B)
immense, (C) enormous 4. (A) scarcity, (C) paucity 5. (A) fleeting, (B) transient
6. (C) scanty, (D) skimpy 7. (B) unnecessary, (D) superfluous 8. (A) generous in
spirit, (D) big-hearted

Words in Context

1. any standard used for making judgments 2. a person of rank, power, or
influence 3. fading fast, like vapor 4. in great and plentiful supply 5. very, very
tiny 6. talk indirectly or in any confusing way; mincing words with someone is
failing to be direct 7. briefness, succinctness 8. big-hearted, forgiving
9. unnecessary, superfluous 10. enormous, huge, impressive

Matching Antonyms

1. enduring, long-lived 2. scanty, minuscule, also meager 3. plentiful amount,
copious 4. superabundance, plentiful amount 5. tiny, minuscule, also meager

LIST 13 (p. 89)

Matching

1. unwanted or unneeded 2. unavoidable 3. opportunistic 4. strenuous
5. insanely idealistic 6. of doubtful authorship 7. commonplace 8. abominable,
appalling

Fill In the Blanks

1. predilection 2. eclectic 3. prodigal 4. legitimate 5. legislate 6. negligible
7. ironic 8. aesthetic

Analogies

1. (D) daydreaming : quixotic :: cleaning house : mundane
   Activity linked to most logical descriptive adjective.

2. (E) bad : heinous :: difficult : arduous

Escalating degree. Bad is much less awful than *heinous*, just as difficult is much less demanding than *arduous*.

3. (B) apocryphal : legend :: fictitious : fable

Logical literary description linked to literary genre. Both legends and fables are apt to be made up—fictitious.

Find the Antonym

1. apocryphal 2. quixotic 3. avoidable 4. desired 5. significant 6. aversion 7. haphazard 8. noble 9. customary 10. mundane 11. parsimonious 12. impractical

LIST 14 (p. 94)

Substitution

1. rhetorical 2. garble 3. diatribe 4. satire 5. blasphemy 6. garrulous 7. jargon 8. indicted 9. tirade 10. slander

True or False

1. T 2. F 3. F 4. T 5. T 6. F 7. T

Matching

1. wordy, garrulous 2. defame, slander (or dishonor or malign) 3. fretful, petulant 4. corrosive, caustic 5. command, legal order 6. questioning, curious 7. defame, dishonor (or malign)

LIST 15 (p. 99)

Words In Context

1. *indifferent* = unconcerned, aloof, unattached, uninterested 2. *capitulate* = yield or give in to what another wants 3. *defer* = put off until another time 4. *innocuous* = harmless 5. *languor* = sluggishness, lethargy 6. *stagnant* = stale, unmoving, inactive 7. *deduced* = concluded or inferred through reasoned thought

Matching

1. (A) vary up or down, (D) come and go 2. (B) suspicious, (C) of doubtful quality 3. (C) wishy-washiness, (D) indecision 4. (A) hesitant, (B) unsure 5. (B) languorous, (D) torpid 6. (C) indefinite, (D) uncertain 7. (A) avoid, (C) circumvent 8. (B) promoting, (D) assisting 9. (C) permeate, (D) diffuse throughout

Find the Synonym

1. evade 2. defer 3. languor 4. innocuous 5. stagnant 6. indifferent 7. tentative 8. capitulate

REVIEW, LISTS 11–15
Analogies

1. (C) vacillate : ambivalence :: blaspheme : irreverence

   Implied comparison. To *vacillate* is to reveal *ambivalence*, just as to *blaspheme* shows *irreverence*.

2. (D) ephemeral : duration :: meager : amount

   Words of measurement in implied comparison. Something that is only *ephemeral* in duration won't last long, just as something *meager* in amount won't last very long either.

3. (B) satire : irony :: tirade : criticism

   Part of a whole or related by definition, maybe even implied comparison! Think of this sentence: *Irony* is basic to *satire*, just as *criticism* is the basis of a *tirade*.

4. (E) reputation : slander :: communication : garble

   Implied comparison. To *slander* a reputation ruins it, just as to *garble* a bit of communication ruins it.

5. (B) spirit : magnanimous :: effort : prodigious

   Relationship of size. A big spirit is a *magnanimous* one, just as a big effort is a *prodigious* one.

Matching

1. (B) give way to 2. (A) hint 3. (C) foil 4. (D) sharpen 5. (A) natural preference
6. (B) demanding 7. (B) fictitious 8. (D) languor 9. (C) beyond question 10. (A) superfluous

Find the Oddball

1. announce 2. adjudicate 3. admonish 4. speech 5. jargon 6. dirty 7. menial
8. vapor 9. unreal 10. goal-oriented 11. supply 12. adorable

Fill In the Blanks

1. waive 2. tentative 3. conducive 4. copious, prodigious 5. prodigal 6. eclectic
7. aesthetic 8. fluctuated, negligible 9. pervasive, deduced 10. vitriolic, vilified
11. diatribe, capitulated, innocuous 12. saturated, clamoring

LIST 16 (p. 108)

Fill In the Blanks

1. enjoins 2. undermined 3. extorting 4. solicitous 5. emanates 6. rescinded
7. extricate 8. emulate 9. expedite 10. subjugating 11. relegate 12. enhances

Rhyme Time

1. repudiate 2. hamper, relegated 3. rescind, enhance 4. squander 5. extort

Matching

1. facilitate 2. squander 3. ask for 4. hamper 5. weaken gradually 6. seep out
7. forbid 8. try to equal 9. tortuous 10. repeal

LIST 17 (p. 113)

True or False

1. F 2. T 3. T 4. F 5. T 6. F 7. F 8. T 9. T 10. T

Find the Oddball

1. price 2. honor 3. urgency 4. symbiosis 5. master 6. hackneyed 7. aloof

Matching

1. sloth, idleness 2. mercy, lenience 3. a cleansing, a purging 4. wrong
assumption, error 5. obstacle, impediment 6. paradox, irregularity 7. neophyte,
novice 8. convivial, sociable 9. original, new 10. outstandingly bad, flagrant

LIST 18 (p. 118)

Find the Synonyms

1. frivolity 2. amiable 3. jocular (effervescent is okay) 4. dispassionate
5. apathetic 6. effervescent 7. serene 8. benign 9. amity 10. jocular

Fill In the Blanks

1. benign or serene 2. extolled 3. placid 4. effervescence 5. ameliorate
6. frivolous 7. Blithe 8. assuage 9. elation 10. blithe, amiable, or maybe jocular;
appease

Find the Antonyms

1. downcast 2. effervescent 3. irritate 4. dispassionate 5. censure 6. frivolous
7. overwrought

LIST 19 (p. 123)

Words in Context

1. *unsavory* = unappetizing, unappealing, disgusting 2. *inflated* = puffed up,
enlarged 3. *impotent* = powerless, ineffective 4. *partial* = biased, strongly
disposed toward 5. *intangible* = not concrete, impalpable yet real 6. *auspicious*
= favorable, boding well, propitious 7. *indiscriminate* = randomly, without

discrimination 8. *dissent* = disagreement 9. *autocrat* = despot, tyrant, dictator 10. *aristocracy* = ruling class; qualified ones

True or False

1. F   2. T   3. F   4. F (maybe T!)   5. T   6. T (You can guess this one even if you don't know for sure.)   7. T   8. F   9. T   10. T

LIST 20 (p. 128)
Substitution

1. didactic 2. gullible 3. incorrigible 4. inane, wanton 5. tedious 6. docile, pompous 7. officious 8. petty 9. dogmatic 10. insipid

Matching

1. inconstant, changeable 2. naive, ingenuous 3. dull, flavorless 4. pedantic, preachy 5. delinquent, recalcitrant 6. witless, insipid 7. unchecked, inhumane 8. established, traditional 9. compliant, tractable 10. interfering, impertinent

Find the Oddball

1. ugly 2. unsavory 3. biased 4. theoretical 5. moderate 6. fickle

REVIEW LISTS 16–20
ANALOGIES

1. (D) reasoning : fallacious :: judgment : biased

   Implied comparison. The worst kind of reasoning would be *fallacious*, just as the worst kind of judgment would be *biased*.

2. (C) infamy : censure :: virtue : extol

   Cause and effect. Historically, we *censure* infamy, just as we *extol* virtue.

3. (E) pleasant : jocular :: contented : blithe

   Ascending degree.

4. (E) demagogue : sincerity :: neophyte : experience

   Person and missing trait. A *demagogue* usually lacks sincerity, just as a *neophyte* lacks experience.

5. (B) effervescent : elation :: deflated : repudiation

   Cause and effect. The result of elation is an *effervescent* feeling, just as the result of repudiation is a *deflated* feeling.

6. (E) confidence : undermine :: embankment : erode

   Implied comparison. Confidence can be *undermined* in the same way that an embankment is *eroded*. (Very similar processes although one is concrete, the other abstract.)

Matching Antonyms

1. concrete 2. humble 3. carefully controlled 4. hinder 5. aggravate 6. ominous, foreboding 7. agreement 8. engrossing, absorbing 9. ineffective 10. disgrace 11. similarity 12. implicate

Find Those Synonyms

1. hinder, impede 2. repeal, call back 3. enjoin, command 4. tortuous, crooked 5. novice, beginner 6. gregarious, amicable 7. vacillating, inconstant 8. assuage, conciliate 9. unfeeling, apathetic 10. insipid, empty

Good Words Get Around

1. undermining 2. impartial 3. squander 4. alleviates 5. placid 6. frivolous 7. dogmatic 8. petty

LIST 21 (p. 137)
Fill In the Blanks

1. credulous 2. scrupulous 3. Steadfast 4. thrifty, prudence 5. pragmatist 6. exemplary 7. frugality, diligence, prudence, discretion, and thrift, plus probably pragmatism and steadfastness, too—eight virtues in all! 8. parochial (narrow) 9. solemnity, solemn 10. credibility, generic

Add the Synonyms

1. frugal, sparing, provident 2. prudent, also modest 3. parochial 4. exemplary 5. scrupulous 6. steadfast, faithful 7. congenial, with kindred tastes

True or False

1. T 2. F 3. T 4. F (probably) 5. F 6. F 7. T 8. T

LIST 22 (p. 142)
Substitution

1. intercede 2. oblivious 3. cryptic or enigmatic 4. hypothetical 5. chimerical 6. esoteric 7. karma 8. elusive 9. eccentric, precedent 10. chronic, utopia

True or False

1. T 2. T 3. F 4. F 5. F 6. F 7. T

Matching

1. without example, novel 2. perceptive, a seer 3. aberrational, odd 4. undecipherable, enigmatic 5. "out to lunch," clueless 6. intervene, mediate 7. repetitive, long-lasting 8. secondhand, substitutionary 9. ideal, perfect 10. fanciful, imaginary

LIST 23 (p. 147)

Fill-In Chart

1. *vindictive*; dic/dict = say; revengeful, *spiteful* 2. turbulent; turb = agitate; *seething, agitated* 3. *homogeneous*; hom = same, gen = kind; same or alike throughout 4. *animosity*; anim = spirit, soul; enmity, *hatred* 5. *haphazard*; hap = luck, chance; *unplanned, random* 6. *equanimity*; equ = equal, same; anim = spirit, soul; *evenness of disposition, balance* 7. virulent; virus = poison; *noted for fast, powerful, and often fatal progress (virulent disease)* 8. convivial; con = with; viv = life; *party-loving, lively* 9. *ubiquitous*; ubique = everywhere; *omnipresent* 10. precocious; pre = before; coquere = cooked; *mentally ahead of schedule, prematurely bright*

Rhyme Time

1. voluminous 2. voracious, whimsical 3. ubiquitous, "viable" 4. unimpeachable 5. incongruous

Word Analysis

1. precocious 2. incongruous 3. turbulent 4. voracious 5. whimsical 6. vindictive

LIST 24 (p. 152)

Fill In the Blanks

1. extenuating 2. iconoclast 3. unethical 4. kindle 5. elaboration 6. tacit 7. insidious 8. tenuous 9. unscathed 10. propensity

Matching Antonyms

1. honorable 2. peripheral 3. kindle 4. elaborate 5. discord 6. deter 7. spoken 8. precipitate 9. careless 10. traditionalist

Matching

1. caustic, highly critical 2. tendency, inclination 3. around the edge, auxiliary 4. lack of harmony, strife 5. barely perceptible, flimsy 6. discourage, inhibit 7. dangerously alluring, subtle 8. model, admired example 9. impetuous, headlong 10. persistent, most attentive

LIST 25 (p. 157)

Substitution

1. arbitrary 2. desultory 3. detrimental 4. flagrant 5. resigned 6. sporadic 7. capricious 8. blatant 9. inherently 10. incisive

True or False

1. F 2. F 3. F 4. T 5. F 6. F

Matching

1. logical, lucid 2. succinct, brief 3. roundabout, crafty 4. agreeable, well-suited 5. liable, receptive to 6. irrelevant, nonessential 7. inborn, natural 8. "loud," glaring 9. irregular, inconstant 10. despotic, impulsive

REVIEW, LISTS 21–25
Analogies

1. (D) time : anachronistic :: setting : incongruous

   Implied comparison. Something out of place in time is *anachronistic*, just as something out of place in a particular setting appears *incongruous*: it "doesn't fit."

2. (B) prophet : clairvoyant :: paradigm : exemplary

   Person related to most logical trait. A prophet should be *clairvoyant*, just as a *paradigm* should be elemplary.

3. (D) apparent : flagrant :: careful : assiduous

   Ascending degree. *Flagrant* is the extreme of apparent, just as *assiduous* is the extreme of careful.

4. (E) water : turbulent :: thought : incoherent

   Implied comparison. Churning water is *turbulent*, just as churning thought is *incoherent*.

5. (B) appetite : voracious :: apparel : voluminous

   Comparison of size. A big, impressive appetite is often termed *voracious*, just as noticeable clothing that billows about like sails on a ship is termed *voluminous*.

6. (A) extraneous : detail :: peripheral : issue

   Comparison of location or function. An unnecessary detail is *extraneous*, just as an unnecessary issue is *peripheral*.

Find the Oddball

1. brilliant (others related by the root *gen*) 2. prophecy 3. pragmatic 4. running 5. hideous 6. fragile 7. elucidate 8. alternate 9. erroneous 10. indigent 11. inspired 12. reclusive

Who Said That?

1. pious one 2. iconoclast 3. clairvoyant 4. eccentric 5. arbitrary one 6. pragmatist 7. credulous one 8. vindictive one 9. convivial soul

Find the Synonyms
1. congenial, compatible 2. capricious, whimsical 3. desultory, haphazard
4. cryptic, enigmatic 5. frugal, thrifty 6. parochial, narrow 7. flimsy, tenuous
8. tacit, unspoken 9. propensity, tendency 10. chimerical, fanciful

The Root of It All
1. adhesive 2. genius 3. ingenuous 4. gene 5. engender 6. generic 7. disingenuous
8. credible 9. intercede 10. chronic 11. animosity 12.equanimity 13. insidious
14. extenuating 15. incisors

LIST 26 (p. 166)
Fill In the Blanks
1. enervating, exhaust 2. belittle 3. carping 4. bolster 5. infer 6. perceptive
7. depleting (maybe exhausting) 8. incipient 9. facilitate 10. coercion, cajoled

Antonyms
1. undermine 2. replenish 3. extol (also, acclaim) 4. terminal, final 5. hamper,
hinder 6. dull, obtuse 7. energize 8. contain 9. acclaim (extol is okay)

Switcheroo
1. estrangement 2. sponsorship, support 3. exhaustion 4. keenness 5. supporter
6. (rapid) multiplication 7. conclusion, deduction 8. negative criticism
9. wheedling, begging 10. force

LIST 27 (p. 171)
True or False
1. F 2. F 3. T 4. T 5. T 6. T 7. T 8. F 9. T 10. T
Find the Synonyms
1. fantastic, shocking 2. unimaginative, ordinary 3. ludicrous, absurd
4. unchanging, stationary 5. sophisticated, suave 6. obtuse, dull-witted 7. very
clever, insidious 8. dormant, potential 9. inborn, inherent 10. frank, guileless

Substitution
1. prosaic, bizarre 2. urbane, opaque 3. candid, stoic, acrimonious 4. static
(slang usage) 5. zany, futile

LIST 28 (p. 177)
Find the Oddball
1. skillful 2. dangerous 3. charming 4. wary 5. pedestrian

Matching
1. refractory, unruly 2. prudent, watchful 3. unassertive, hestitant 4. outmoded, passé 5. totally accurate, demanding 6. productive, fertile 7. unimaginative, ordinary 8. very noticeable, striking 9. unnecessary, wasteful

Fill In the Blanks
1. quizzical 2. obsolete 3. unassailable 4. salutary 5. reprehensible 6. conspicuous (a literal term, from actual citations) 7. fluent 8. Rigorous 9. mellifluous 10. volatile

LIST 29 (P. 182)
Fill In the Blanks
1. demeanor 2. nonchalantly 3. authoritarian 4. perfidy 5. erratic 6. contrite 7. spurious 8. austere 9. altruism 10. conciliatory

Who Said That?
1. an austere person 2. the provincial 3. the brusque type 4. an altruist 5. a partisan 6. an infidel 7. the authoritarian 8. a perfidious one 9. a nonchalant one

True or False
1. T 2. F 3. T 4. T 5. F 6. T 7. T 8. F

LIST 30 (p. 187)
Words in Context
1. *clandestine* = secret, surreptitious; *furtive* = on the sly, secret; *apprehensive* = worried, fearful of something bad 2. *depraved* = morally corrupt; *deleterious* = injurious, harmful 3. *decadence* = decay of moral standards and ethical conduct 4. *caustic* = biting, cutting, corrosive; *cynic* = person who distrusts human nature and views people pessimistically 5. *crass* = lacking good taste, crude, vulgar 6. *guileless* = lacking guile or trickery, ingenuous, open 7. *rebellious* = stubbornly resistant to authority 8. *negligence* = lack of care and attention, neglect; *morosely* = sullenly, gloomily

Matching Synonyms
1. secret 2. to go apart 3. biting, corrosive 4. different 5. foreboding 6. deterioration 7. in poor taste 8. spoiling for a fight 9. deceit 10. pessimistic

Rhyme Time
1. morose 2. depravity 3. furtive 4. bellicose (maybe belligerent, but it has too many syllables) 5. diverged

REVIEW, LISTS 26–30
Analogies

1. (D) document : spurious :: passport : false

   Implied comparison. A fake document is often termed *spurious*, just as a fake passport is usually termed *false.*

2. (C) resources : deplete :: strength : exhaust

   Implied comparison. To use up nearly all of your resources is to *deplete* them (common usage), just as using up nearly all of your strength is to *exhaust* it.

3. (E) carping : alienation :: negligence : decadence

   Cause and effect. *Carping* (repeated crisicism) often leads to alienation, just as negligence may lead to *decadence* (deterioration and decay).

4. (B) misanthrope : cynical :: stoic : impassive

   Person and most logical trait.

5. (A) subtle : covert :: flagrant : conspicuous

   Synonymous or by-definition relationship. Something *subtle* is by its nature a covert thing, just as something *flagrant* is bound to be conspicuous.

6. (B) partisan : aloof :: infidel : loyal

   Person and least likely trait/missing trait. A *partisan* will never remain aloof, just as an *infidel* will not remain loyal (to whatever group he once belonged to).

Matching Antonyms
1. laudable 2. provincial 3. guileful 4. belittle 5. deleterious 6. docile 7. learned, acquired 8. self-indulgence 9. vital 10. conciliatory 11. coerce 12. self-absorption

Matching
1. orally skilled, graceful 2. potential, dormant 3. unassertive, hesitant 4. remorseful, repentant 5. gross, tasteless 6. surreptitious, clandestine 7. perceptive, pointed 8. conclude, deduce 9. pedestrian, everyday 10.autocratic, despotic

Fill In the Blanks
1. prolific, diverse 2. static 3. facilitate, futile 4. erratic, aberration 5. circumspect 6. morose, rigorous 7. denouncing, caustic 8. bellicose, advocate

True or False
1. T 2. F 3. T 4. T 5. T 6. F

INDEX OF WORDS AND ROOTS

The words and roots taught in this book are presented here in alphabetical order for ease of reference. Following each word is the number of the list, or chapter, in which it appears. Roots are in bold type.

Peterson's unplugged

graduate programs

distance learning

adult education

executive training

colleges and universities

private secondary schools

internships and careers

study-abroad programs

financial aid/scholarships

summer programs

Peterson's quality on every page!

For more than three decades, we've offered a complete selection of books to guide you in all of your educational endeavors. You can find our vast collection of titles at your local bookstore or online at **petersons.com**.

High school student headed for college?

Busy professional interested in distance learning?

Parent searching for the perfect private school or summer camp?

Human resource manager looking for executive education programs?

AOL Keyword: Petersons
Phone: 800-338-3282